P V

 St. Louis Community College

Forest Park
Florissant Valley
Meramec

Instructional Resources
St. Louis, Missouri

A Guide
to
Research in
Gerontology

A GUIDE TO RESEARCH IN GERONTOLOGY

STRATEGIES AND RESOURCES

Dorothea R. Zito and
George V. Zito

Foreword by
MARTA DOSA

Greenwood Press
New York · Westport, Connecticut · London

Library of Congress Cataloging-in-Publication Data

Zito, Dorothea R.
  A guide to research in gerontology : strategies and resources /
Dorothea R. Zito and George V. Zito : foreword by Marta Dosa.
    p. cm.
  Bibliography: p.
  Includes index.
  ISBN 0-313-25904-6 (lib. bdg. : alk. paper)
  1. Reference books—Gerontology.   2. Gerontology—Bibliography.
3. Gerontology—Information services.   4. Gerontology—Library
resources.   I. Zito, George V.   II. Title.
Z7164.04Z57   1989
[HQ1061]
016.3052′6—dc19   88-17773

British Library Cataloguing in Publication Data is available.

Library of Congress Catalog Card Number: 88-17773
ISBN: 0-313-25904-6

First published in 1988

Greenwood Press, Inc.
88 Post Road West, Westport, Connecticut 06881

Printed in the United States of America

The paper used in this book complies with the
Permanent Paper Standard issued by the National
Information Standards Organization (Z39.48-1984).

10 9 8 7 6 5 4 3 2 1

For our children,
Darlene, Robin, Thea and Pamela

CONTENTS

CONTENTS

FIGURES AND TABLES

FIGURES

TABLES

FOREWORD

The information environment of gerontology is shaped by economic, social, and political considerations. Information specialists, gerontologists, and all other users of the gerontological literature face a formidable maze of societal activities and relationships that produce and transmit information relevant to aging. Of the numerous forces that characterize gerontological information, we may identify three major features that especially affect literature resources and searches.

1. Information emanates from societywide spheres of policy, research, practice, advocacy, and education.
   a) The policy literature includes congressional, state, and local legislative processes and regulatory action; testimonies of special interest groups; and policies of organizations and corporations in the private sector.
   b) The research literature reflects the cross-disciplinary nature of basic and applied investigations ranging over a large number of disciplines and professions encompassing the physical, life and social sciences, law, medicine, social work, nursing, management, and so forth. The humanities also make their own invaluable research contributions to our understanding of aging.

    c) Professional practice, representing the front line work of service providers, planners, and administrators, produces data, reports, and surveys—much of which is difficult to locate. Components of the "aging network" of agencies at the federal, state, and local levels are prolific producers of documents and other sources.

    d) Advocacy cuts across the domains of public and special interests in the economics and politics of aging. Information from and about the ever-growing importance of the elderly population and the families of the frail elderly is indispensable in research and social action.

    e) Educators and learners at all levels engaged in formal, nonformal, and informal programs create a multiplicity of information resources. In the industrial sector, examples comprise staff training and demonstration of new technology and processes as well as retirement counseling; in the private nonprofit sector, the training of personnel and client groups; in the public sector, the ongoing preparation of policy-makers, regulators, and implementers; and in academic institutions, formal education and continuing education programs.

2. In gerontology we also recognize the significance of the transmission of research findings into decision-making, program and curriculum innovation, and technology development. Without this information flow and feedback to researchers, the application of new knowledge will lag behind.

3. The literature of gerontology has certain attributes that affect access to sources and channels of access.

    a) Information resources pertaining to social, economic, legal, medical, psychological, and other problems in aging and in society's response to these needs, are scattered in the literatures of many knowledge fields as well as in emerging multidisciplinary areas such as medical geriatrics, sociolinguistics, environmental psychology, intergroup behavior, the politics of public participation or medical technology.

    b) Barrier-free access to computerized information systems and the content of information are often affected by the policies of information producers in the public and private sectors.

c) The understanding of what kinds of scientific, legal, and administrative facts are needed by various information-user groups in gerontology is growing at a very slow rate.

d) In gerontology, as in other societal knowledge fields, there is a need for objective scientific and validated information as well as for the subjective opinion literature of various social groups.

These factors affecting the need for gerontological information and the use of the literature present a considerable challenge to researchers, policy-makers, practitioners, advocates, educators, and learners. Librarians and other information specialists whose roles are to act as intermediaries between resources and users, face the same challenge, with the added responsibility to select the most appropriate sources and interpret their use. Drawing on their knowledge and experience in information service and sociological research, respectively, Dorothea and George Zito have provided an excellent guide that will enable information users and intermediaries to meet this challenge.

A Guide to Research in Gerontology will be useful not only for researchers but for all participants in the far-flung gerontological community. The eminent value of this guide lies in the conceptualization of gerontological knowledge and its use, the lucid organization of reference tools and access points, and the effective communication of strategies. This is a tool for linking knowledge to its applications through effective literature searches.

There are numerous specific features embedded in this volume that merit recognition, and the following serve as examples. The literature is placed into a social context, helping the reader to understand how various disciplines and their literatures interrelate. The scope of coverage is as comprehensive and balanced as a guide in an area constantly in flux can provide. The compilation and interpretation of sources is based on thorough scholarship. The presentation of the material is systematic, enhanced by figures and illustrations of use. Guidance is provided to optimal approaches in literature searching, and annotations give practical keys to the content of tools. Other benefits of this reference source will be discovered by its users.

Dorothea and George Zito have constructed a unique guide to the literature of aging which gives us not only publications and skills in locating information, but also a greater appreciation of the complex social nature of gerontology.

Marta Dosa
Professor
School of Information Studies
Syracuse University

ACKNOWLEDGMENTS

The authors would like to acknowledge the students, faculty, and other professionals working in the field of gerontology for the many insights they have provided to the problems associated with searching for information on aging. By clarifying their problems for us, it became clear that there are many taken-for-granted assumptions of specialists that are not quite so evident to those most in need of their services. Among the many who have provided encouragement to us in this present endeavor, we would like to offer our special thanks to Marta Dosa, Walter Beattie, Neal Bellos, Myron Miller, Erdman Palmore, Rose Tout, Anne Panzarella, and Cindy Lange.

A Guide
to
Research in
Gerontology

1

INTRODUCTION: THE COMPLEXITIES OF THE GERONTOLOGICAL LITERATURE

The growing expansion of the world's older population is reflected in a tremendous increase in the literature concerned with aging. This literature comes from many different sources and incorporates diverse nomenclatures from many relatively unrelated disciplines. Changes in the age structure of society has brought about social changes, and this is reflected in an increased concern in research to understand not only the social, but the psychological and physiological processes of aging. This has increased both the number and kinds of publications. In technical journals, the popular press and magazines, and wherever information is transmitted to the public and to researchers and practitioners, the impact has been particularly strong. Practitioners have been able to fuse basic and applied research to provide more insightful applications of research to the care of the elderly, further increasing the volume of literature in all areas of study.

It is the purpose of this book to make this literature available to prospective users. Although designed primarily for information specialists, it will prove useful to students and professionals in a wide variety of academic disciplines. They have increasingly turned to studies of the elderly in attempting to understand social and personal problems that are only in the process of emerging at the end of this century. Social workers and persons in the health-care professions will find it particularly useful for locating sources of information on specific subjects related to aging.

In the United States, the segment of the population 65 years and over has been growing at a dramatic rate. According to the U.S. Bureau of the Census, this age group numbered 12.4 million in 1950 and by 1980 had more than doubled in size, to 25.7 million. It is projected to reach 35 million by the year 2000 and 64 million in 2030.

Of particular significance is the fact that the U.S. population aged 75 years and older, those most in need of health care and services, is expected to peak between the years 2020 and 2040. An estimated 30 million persons in the old-old age group (as this group is now referred to) is projected for the year 2030. For the first time in the history of the United States, American society is faced with the likelihood that approximately one-fifth of its population will be in the over 65 age group. As the size of this older population increases, problems related to this group become more salient, opening up vast areas of new research.

Gerontology, as the study of both the causes and the consequences of aging—the physiological, psychosocial, political, and environmental factors that affect human beings at a particular stage in the life cycle—must meet the challenges this change represents.

The knowledge base of gerontology comprises information from almost all disciplines and can be found in most of the traditional fields of academic study and human-service practice. Physiologists examine aging in relation to the functioning ability of the bodily organs. The psychologist studies the changes in cognitive functioning, while the architect examines the environment in relation to the structures in both institutions and community housing that increase the quality of life for aging individuals. Human-service workers and health professionals consider the health and maintenance of an advancing aging population, while the economists view the financial impact this population has on both the individual and the state.

This has not always been the case. Aging research during the early 1900s was undertaken primarily in the area of plants and animals, and human aging seems to have been generally neglected. The earliest reliable literature concentrated on a few publications such as Minot's *The Problems of Age, Growth, and Death* (1908), Mitchenkoff's *The Prolongation of Life* (1908), Child's *Senescence and Rejuvenescence* (1915), and Pearl's *Biology of Death* (1922). In contrast, the late 1970s and early 1980s have seen the emergence of a vast amount of literature on human aging. Aside from the increase in the number of monographs, there has been an extensive increase in the number of highly specialized journals on aging and information resources, as well as a computerized database. Periodicals have emerged in the area of housing for the elderly, nutrition, religion, and social work, to name a few. Indexes such as the *Index to Periodical Literature on Aging* and Excerpta Medica's *Gerontology and Geriatrics* provide access to the literature in social gerontology, allied health, and geriatrics. *Ageline*, developed by the American Association of Retired Persons (AARP), is a computerized database devoted to aging literature. Despite the recognition that the field of gerontology requires its own body of information resources, publication continues in traditional places that may be unfamiliar to workers and researchers in the gerontology field. There remains an abundance of literature on aging that lies outside the specialized resources in gerontology. Information written before the introduction of such specialized resources are scattered throughout the resources of other disciplines, and some disciplines can be expected to continue to publish in this area if they deal with the human condition.

In an era of specialization, the gerontologist must "despecialize" if he or she is to obtain the maximum amount of information from a variety of disciplines with a minimum amount of time and energy. Figure 1 suggests what some of these disciplines are and some of their interests. All the human studies are included and each contains a wealth of information related to the subject of aging. If the primary function of information is to increase knowledge by providing a basis for understanding new phenomena, the gerontologist must be able to track down such information wherever it may exist. Only then can we fully understand the problems and processes of aging and their impact on both the individual and society as a whole.

To appropriately cover the many sources of data in gerontol-

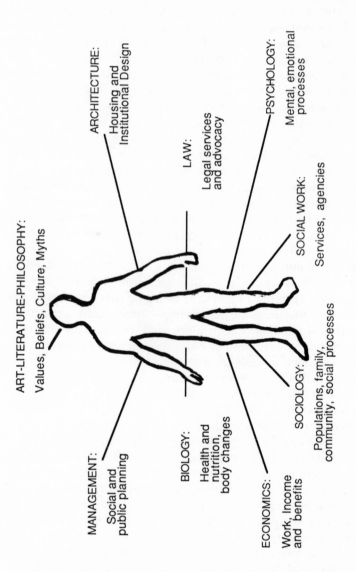

Figure 1
The Human Sciences and Gerontology

ART-LITERATURE-PHILOSOPHY:
Values, Beliefs, Culture, Myths

ARCHITECTURE:
Housing and
Institutional Design

PSYCHOLOGY:
Mental, emotional
processes

LAW:
Legal services
and advocacy

SOCIAL WORK:
Services, agencies

MANAGEMENT:
Social and
public planning

BIOLOGY:
Health and
nutrition,
body changes

ECONOMICS:
Work, Income
and benefits

SOCIOLOGY:
Populations, family,
community, social processes

ogy requires the ability to use all the information resources available not only in the gerontology literature, but in other disciplines as well. It requires those seeking this information to search for information systematically rather than haphazardly. Understanding the way information is produced, organized, and distributed provides a greater access to data with a reduction in the amount of time and energy spent on retrieving what is essential. Developing search strategies and techniques will direct the information searcher toward the most relevant information resources wherever they exist, in the gerontology literature or in the literature of other disciplines.

The present volume is intended to expand skills in locating information in the area of gerontology and geriatrics and to provide a wide range of information resources on the subjects. It is assumed that the searcher has access to a university library and local and regional public libraries. The use of a computer terminal or of a personal (or "micro") computer may also be useful, particularly if the most recent information is required in the shortest possible time.

The text has been organized as an information resource for information specialists but is also useful to students, researchers, practitioners, and other professionals in gerontology and geriatrics. It may be read as a text but is especially useful as a working reference guide to locating the sources of information dealing with the aged and with aging.

Figure 2 illustrates how the text is organized. Chapters 2 and 3 and Appendix A form the central core of the text. Chapter 2 sets forth the procedures to employ when searching for gerontological materials and its methods are applicable to all the chapters that follow. Appendix A is a general reading list on aging, classified by subject. Newcomers to the field as well as those searching for an initial orientation to some segment of the literature will find the appendix particularly useful. Chapter 3 discusses the varieties of information resources in gerontology, and is a bridge to the more specialized chapters that follow. Appendix C lists the important journals that most often provide the primary source materials. Both Chapter 5, "Indexes and Abstracts," and Chapter 7, "Computerized Infor-

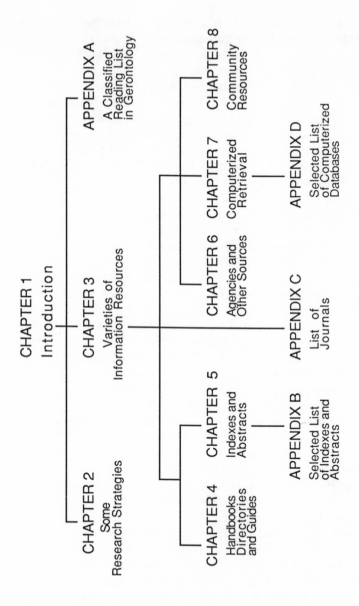

Figure 2
Organization of the Text

mation Retrieval Systems," are supplied with appendices that provide access to these areas. Chapters 6 and 8 may serve as guides to sources of information on two often neglected resource areas, agencies and the local community.

2

RESEARCH STRATEGIES

Time and energy are valuable components of everyone's life. Students have deadlines for term papers, professionals must carry out their daily responsibilities as well as publish papers or books, develop new projects, and keep abreast of new developments in their fields. In today's world the "bottom line" is information, and information then becomes power. But it is not information per se that constitutes power: it is only access to the relevant information at the relevant time.

More and more information is being generated. On-line computer databases can provide information in a matter of seconds on almost every conceivable subject. However, too much information at one time can be overwhelming and confusing. Today, more than at any other time, there is a need for developing strategies for efficiently locating information in order to provide ready answers to the many questions that are being posed.

The aim of developing such strategies is to go from a question that needs to be answered to the retrieval of documents that provide an answer or answers to that question. This is suggested in Figure 3. In addition, planning a search strategy enables the searcher to clarify the problem and to focus on its key elements. Too often, the initial emphasis is placed on the information resources available rather than on the mental or

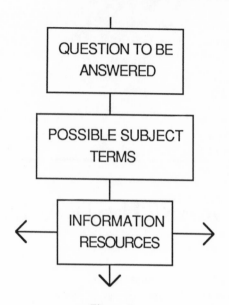

Figure 3
Research Questions and Information Resources

"mind" work involved. Only after the question has been for-mulated do the resource tools for locating documents become truly invaluable. Essentially, it is necessary to know what to look for, where to look for it, and how to retrieve the docu-ments once they have been located.

All too often the tendency in searching for information is to plunge bravely into the unknown waters. Scanning a library card catalog for books or poring through journals for relevant articles is not unusual. This may, in some cases, retrieve infor-mation on the topic. It may by accident locate a bibliography, a key article, a literature review, or a text on the subject; simi-larly, it may mislead the searcher to the false conclusion that there is no published information on the topic. This careless entry into the information resources may sometimes be conve-nient as a preliminary search of the subject, perhaps to help determine what terms may be useful as a preliminary search for the possible selection of a research topic. Depending on the documents retrieved, the depth of the information needed, and

the time restrictions, this may or may not answer one's imme-
diate information needs. Usually it does not. Developing a search
strategy for retrieving information is a much more efficient and
less time-consuming method of locating relevant documents. It
is, indeed, the only method employed by professional information specialists.

As in any research effort, it is difficult to pose the initial
question. Trying various subject terms as possible keys helps
clarify the problem, or perhaps helps restate it in other, more
manageable, terms. Only when some decisions have been made
with respect to possible subject terms should recourse be at-
tempted to the information resources. As Figure 3 suggests,
these resources lead in several possible directions.

Planning a search strategy enables the searcher to clarify and
focus on the key elements involved in the proposed research
question. When done correctly, it will lead to the specific information resources that will point to the documentation that answers the research question. Essentially, it is necessary to know
what to look for, where to look for it, and how to retrieve the
document or documents once they have been located.

Knowing where you are headed in a search for information
can be compared to taking a trip to Boston for the first time to
attend a gerontology conference. You may know that Boston is
north or south of where you live and head in that general direction. You may or may not arrive at your destination, or you
may arrive too late to attend the conference. Having a vague
notion of a search topic and heading to the nearest library or
doing a computer database search is similar to taking the scenic
route in the direction of Boston. It may provide you with a
great deal of interesting information that may or may not be
relevant to your topic, and cost you both time and, in the case
of a computer database search, money.

Information search strategies may be simple or complex. They
may take a variety of forms depending on the topic under investigation, knowledge of available information resources, and
the depth of information required to satisfactorily answer the
research question. A strategy may begin with a library search
for general texts on the topic under investigation, scanning a
specialized journal in gerontology, or using a handbook that

provides an overview of the topic. Or it may begin with scanning a compiled bibliography, index, or abstract, or possibly with an informal discussion with a colleague. However, in all cases, there must be a question to be answered. Knowing where you are headed requires a knowledge of what you are looking for and how you can locate the information you require. Clearly defining the topic of an information search is the key element to locating relevant data.

Assuming you have already selected a more or less general area of research to investigate, you should begin by highlighting what you consider to be the key issues. Try to ask such questions as *who, what, when, where,* and *why*? *Who* are you concerned about? *What* are you concerned about and *why*? In gerontology, the first question, the *who* usually amounts to trying to define the particular segment of the population you are interested in. Although the population members are all "aged," they may be the *frail* elderly, the *rural* elderly, or the *urban* elderly. They may be the *minority aged*. These are some of the possible "subject terms" of Figure 3. The exact specification of the subject term is extremely important, because it helps to minimize or eliminate the accumulation of irrelevant data.

The next question to ask may be, *where* is the population of the elderly that is of interest to us located. They may reside in the United States or they may be in more specialized locations such as in the community or in a nursing home. They may be the frail elderly living in the community. What do you want to know about this group? Your question may center on the lack of social and health-care services for the frail elderly living in the community, or how the frail or minority elderly can be helped to stay in the community through the use of support services. Analysis of the characteristics of the population under study helps to clarify the issues involved in your search question, which is now seen as "Can the provision of social and health services maintain the frail elderly in the community?"

Specific questions lead to more precise information gathering by focusing on the elements of the research question that guide the searcher to relevant data. Considering the frail elderly, for example, "What are the problems of the frail elderly living in the community and what types of service would be necessary to maintain them in their own homes? Have other programs been developed in this area?" Here the key subject terms are *frail elderly, community,* and *community services.*

While you are doing the "mind" work in your search strategy, allow for variations in the amount of material available by noting ways to broaden or narrow your search for information. Being prepared for the inevitable false conclusion that "there is too much information on the topic," or its companion "there is no information at all on the topic," can save time locating data. Information on housing for the elderly will retrieve a vast number of documents but this may be narrowed by reducing the categories of the population to those of the *disabled elderly* or limited to *urban* or *congregate housing.* Information on the black elderly and housing can, on the other hand, be broadened to include minority elderly.

After the question has been fairly well clarified in your mind, write it out in a short paragraph or two. Stating the question in writing forces you to concentrate on the areas of information that will enable you to answer the question. Figure 3 may look overly simplistic, but it is not. Writing out what you understand to be the question, then writing a list of subject terms, and finally writing the possible information resources that might yield an answer to the question tends to fix the problem for the moment and allows you to consider alternate possibilities before you begin the search.

The key to success in conducting an information search is often in the selection of those subject terms initially used to begin the search. Subject terms are those words or phrases used to group information on similar topics. The library classification system, for example, is a method of grouping information by similar subjects, as well as a system for locating documents on the shelves of the library. Indexes and abstracts, bibliographies, or the index in the back of a book (including this one) all use subject terms to locate information. An index may use the terms *aged, elderly, older adults,* or *gerontology* to group information on older persons. A text on aging will yield narrower terms such as *sensory processes,* which include vision, hearing, and other senses. A search for information on an older person's sense of taste and smell may not retrieve very much information; however, broadening the subject to *sensory processes* may provide more extensive data that include information on the sense of taste and smell.

Next, select and list the subject terms that describe or define the issues in your question allowing for both broad and narrow terms. In gerontology the key term is the word or phrase used to define the population in the older age groups. This is particularly important when you are searching for information resources outside the gerontology literature. The Library of Congress uses the term *aging* to compile literature in gerontology. The ERIC–CIJE index and abstracting services use the term *older adult;* other indexes and abstracts may use the term *elderly.* The term *aged* or *aging* (or even *ageing*) may, however, include information from birth to old age. Other terms used may include *senior citizens, retirees, gerontology,* and *geriatrics.* Many indexes will include a *see* or *see also* note to direct the user to the standardized term for aging information or related subject terms. The subject terms represent the major point of access to the literature on aging.

As you begin your search for documents you may want to delete terms and add more specific or standardized terms that are used in gerontology. An index in gerontology may choose to place all documents related to housing the elderly under the general term *housing;* however, another index may choose to separate the information into more specific subject areas. *Current Literature on Aging,* for example, which abstracts newly published books and journal articles in the field of social gerontology, uses specific terminology in grouping the literature. The term *housing* is used together with *congregate housing, granny flats, retirement communities,* or *shared housing.* Information on elder abuse may be listed as elder abuse, abuse of the elderly, or battered elderly. Searching for historical information may sometimes require using terms that may seem obsolete today. Information on the black elderly in a historical perspective (for example) may require using the term *Negro* or *colored.* Because terms may vary with indexes and subject bibliographies and change over time, a list of alternative terms reduces the danger of overlooking what may be key information sources. Having a list of alternative terms keeps you from having to "go back to the drawing board" if there is too much or too little information available.

A useful resource for selecting terms in gerontology is published by the National Institutes of Health titled *Age Words: A Glossary on Health and Aging.* It is a collection of common terms used by gerontologists. Terms are defined with an emphasis consistent with common usage. The *Encyclopedia of Aging*, edited by George Maddox, provides a more extensive view of subject areas in gerontology and geriatrics and has the advantage of providing authoritative authors who define the topics as well as supply bibliographic sources. Because libraries all use subject headings to classify documents in their collection, the *Library of Congress Subject Headings* available in most college and university libraries can act as a guide for selecting appropriate terminology. Often an index publication, such as *ERIC*, will provide a thesaurus of terms applicable to gerontology. And, as a last resort, there is the index in the back of a general text on aging.

Up to this point, most of the research strategy has been mental work and can be accomplished at the desk. The next step is to consider those information resources that can provide the information you are searching for. Figure 4 suggests what these may be.

Information can be in the form of research studies, reports, government documents, statistical data, model programs, or theoretical information. It can be located in a variety of information resources. These may be primary, secondary, or tertiary sources (see Chapter 3). Focus on the source material. Who or what would provide information on the question and how would they treat the topic? Defining the kinds of information needed to answer your question leads to the selection of tools to retrieve the sought-after data.

Theoretical or research studies are more likely to be found in the *Journal of Gerontology* or *Research on Aging;* whereas model programs are often found in periodicals aimed at the professional working in the field. The professional journals *Activities, Adaptations & Aging* and *Physical and Occupational Therapy in Geriatrics* will contain articles on model programs, case studies, or therapy programs. The *Index to Periodical Literature on Aging* as

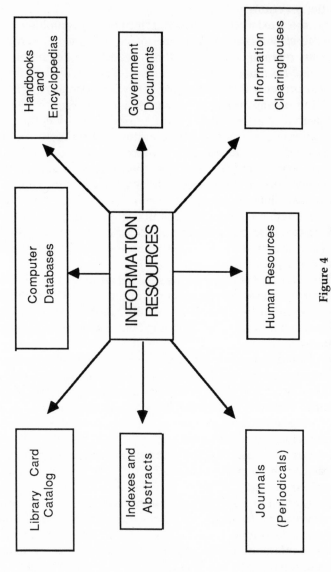

Figure 4
Kinds of Information Resources

well as the *Current Literature on Aging* will, for example, include some government documents or statistical information; however, more extensive information may be found in the *Monthly Catalog of U.S. Government Documents*, or U.S. Bureau of the Census reports. The library card catalog may retrieve the text *Statistical Handbook on Aging Americans* edited by Frank L. Schick, which presents the most recent statistical data as of December 1985 on older Americans under the subject heading "Aging—Statistics."

Scanning sources such as journals appropriate to the topic may yield valuable resources; however, using indexes and abstracts, bibliographies, and handbooks saves time and covers more territory. Although gerontology and geriatric indexes and abstracts, bibliographies, and on-line computer databases all provide data related to aging, it is frequently necessary to enter the resources of other disciplines. Noting the main subject areas of your search and the issues involved guides you to tools in other disciplines that can provide more extensive data.

Identifying the scope of your topic determines which discipline would most likely contain information on the subject. It may be useful to consider Figure 1 again to keep the areas of specialization uppermost in your mind. Although the *Journal of Housing for the Elderly* will contain data related to housing and the physical environment of the elderly, the dates of material it includes are no earlier than 1983, when the journal began its publication. More specific information on the design of architectural structures to accommodate the elderly may require searching architectural journals. Information on the effects of retirement may be included in *Psychological Abstracts*, *Sociological Abstracts*, or *Business Periodicals Index* depending on the approach to the topic of retirement. Data on the emotional and social effects may be located in *Psychological Abstracts* and in *Sociological Abstracts*. Information on the financial and economic effects may be found in the *Business Periodicals Index*. Table 1, for example, shows some of the possible sources in other disciplines that one may employ, when searching for information on retirement.

Focusing on the scope of information contained in the resource material will reduce both the time and frustration in-

Table 1
Sources of Information on Retirement

ECONOMICS
American Economic Review
United States Banker
Dun's Review

EMPLOYMENT BENEFITS
Monthly Labor Review
Employees Benefit Plan Review
Pension World
Social Security Bulletin
Pensions and Investments
National Underwriter
Benefits International

BUSINESS
Harvard Business
Business Week
Business Horizon
Nation's Business
Black Enterprise
Business Insurance

COUNSELING
Journal of Employment
Counseling
International Journal of
   Guidance and Counseling
Vocational Counseling Quarterly
Business Insurance

MANAGEMENT
International Management
Administrative Management
Defense Management Journal

PERSONNEL
Personnel
Personnel and Guidance
Personnel Administration

GERONTOLOGY
Aging and Work
Gerontologist
Journal of Gerontology
Journal of Gerontological Nursing
Aging and Human Development
Experimental Aging and Research
Educational Gerontology

EDUCATION
Adult Leadership
Adult Education
Educational and Research Methods

SOCIAL
Social Casework
Social Work
Family Coordinator
American Sociological Review
Sociology of Work and Occupations

volved in the information search. Searching for information on the effects of Alzheimer's disease on short-term memory in *Psychological Abstracts* may cover the clinical and neurological studies of the disease. If you are looking for information that is less clinical, the *Cumulative Index to Nursing & Allied Health* may provide more relevant information. If there is a roadblock to information in one area, take a different route. The large quantity of information available today can be seen in a positive way, rather than being looked on as something overwhelming. The situation becomes defined as "if there is so much information, then I must be able to locate what I need." The question of *where* can be answered through a variety of sources: the reference librarian, the library card catalog, colleagues, and general reference texts to sources of information.

The amount of time allotted to gathering information is very often the most important criterion. Try not to continually "reinvent the wheel"! Look for shortcuts. Locating an information center, for example, may result in obtaining unpublished bibliographies that can be very useful. The National Clearinghouse on Aging in Washington, D.C., and the National Institute on Aging Information Center in Silver Springs, Maryland, provide extensive literature for the gerontological communities. The NRTA–AARP National Gerontology Resource Center in Washington, D.C., will not only provide information but may also furnish the names and addresses of agencies that can supply information in specialized areas such as arthritis, hospice care, or legal services. The essential step, however, in all areas of information searching, is to know what you are searching for and the nature of the question that has been posed.

Nondocumentary sources should not be overlooked as possible information tools. It is possible to locate experts in the field that can be contacted by telephone when necessary. These are listed in directories. The Gerontological Society of America publishes *Who's Who in Gerontology* (see Chapter 4). This publication contains a list of its members with their names, addresses, and specialized areas in gerontology. Information centers can provide compiled bibliographies or pamphlets on a topic. The Nutrition Information and Resource Center at The Pennsylvania State University provides answers to questions and re-

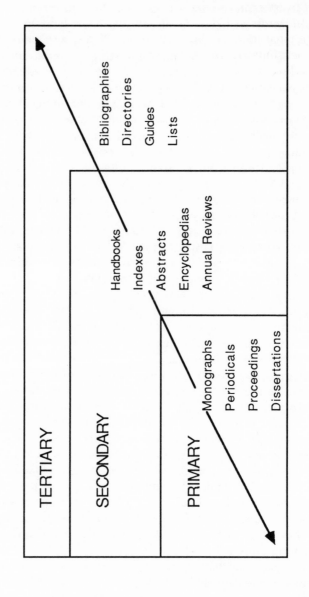

Figure 5
Primary, Secondary, and Tertiary Sources of Information

ferral to other information resources. The *Directory of Gerontological Libraries and Information Centers* by H. Jean Owens lists
institutional libraries that have a specific gerontological focus.
A subject index in the back of the directory includes such areas
as psychology and sociology, rehabilitation, minority aging, and
audiovisual materials. All such steps save time in doing the
initial work of compiling information sources. The aim of such
resource centers and information resource tools is to reduce the
time and frustration that may accompany a search for information.

Figure 5 groups information in terms of primary, secondary,
and tertiary sources.

As the arrow suggests, one may move back and forth among
primary, secondary, and tertiary sources in searching for specific informational data. However, the most efficient retrieval is
obtained when the process that produces the information is re-
versed. This is explained further in the next chapter.

REFERENCES

National Institute on Aging. *Age Words: A Glossary on Health and Aging.*
Bethesda, Md.: National Institutes of Health, 1986.

*Thesaurus of Aging Terminology: Ageline Database on Middle Age and Ag-
ing.* 3d ed. Washington, D.C.: American Association of Retired
Persons, 1986.

3

VARIETIES OF
INFORMATION
SOURCES

In a field such as gerontology, understanding the ways in which information is produced, organized, and distributed allows for greater accessibility to the information sought. It is virtually impossible, especially in a multidisciplinary field, to remember the multiple information resource tools that can provide greater and more efficient access to the wide range of literature involved. However, knowing the way information is arranged allows us to make certain assumptions that can speed up the retrieval of the desired material. This chapter will be concerned with the ways in which information originates and is organized and arranged. This will lead the searcher to the types of resource tools that provide access to the desired documents.

Published literature can be placed into four main categories or types, namely (1) primary, (2) secondary, (3) tertiary, and (4) nondocumentary. These are technically termed *information resource types*. Although some documents may overlap these categories, fitting into more than just one type, this does not reduce the usefulness of this basic hierarchical scheme or of keeping it in mind before beginning a search.

A researcher developing research projects, initiating new programs, or engaged in scientific experiments depends to a great extent on past research in the field in which he or she is working. The published results of such past research comprise *primary sources of data.* The person developing new research projects hopes to develop additional primary data as a result of his or her efforts, but requires the published efforts of previous investigators to build on and extend. Knowledge builds on knowledge, and information builds on information.

Such *primary sources of information,* then, consist of original reports of research, usually published by an individual researcher or a group of researchers who have worked as a team. These primary sources take various forms; they may be articles or papers in the journals of learned societies (professional societies in academic disciplines), monographs, theses, dissertations, or government reports. Primary *data* are usually contained in such primary *sources.* Usually, in seeking information, one wishes to find primary sources in order to find the primary data. It is the data that most often provide the answer to the question posed by the searcher. Primary data, however, are scattered among many publications, and these publications are not organized into any single reference source, making it difficult and time consuming to locate.

The problem may be compared to looking for a pair of bedroom slippers in a large department store. You may travel randomly through many departments on every floor, hoping to spot a pair fortuitously, or you may look for an information booth or wall directory for the floor that sells bedroom slippers. The latter procedure, although better than the first, may not always provide the answer, however. Are bedroom slippers located in the shoe department or the lingerie department? Are they considered lounge wear? The specific category used by the store to classify bedroom slippers is unknown to you. If the wall directory does not list bedroom slippers as such, you may need to go to a nondocumentary source of information, such as a salesperson. He or she should know how the store classifies the merchandise it sells. If the salesperson doesn't, another nondocumentary source, perhaps the floor manager, does know. Of course, it would help you find the slippers on your own if you knew beforehand what system of organization the store employed in placing its sales items on the shelves. You are able to find books in a library because you have some idea of how the Library of Congress classification system works. If you know how the item got where it is you can retrieve it quicker. In much the same way, knowing the way information is produced and then organized allows for its more efficient retrieval.

As we noted earlier, the author of a book, a research article, or a dissertation produces an original work, a *primary source* of information. These contain *primary data* which are scattered through many publications. Sometimes some of the primary sources that are related to each other in topic are republished as anthologies or collections, or appear in handbooks (see Chapter 4). All such publications are considered *secondary sources* because they are not the original (or primary) publications. Secondary sources also include certain other publications such as indexes and abstracts (see Chapter 5 and Appendix B), which provide means of accessing the primary sources. An index lists the primary sources and sometimes includes secondary sources as well, but limits itself to citations without reprinting any of the original texts. Abstracts are short accounts of what is contained in the document cited. A computerized database (see Chapter 7 and Appendix D) is really only an electronic index. Figure 6 illustrates this discussion.

To go one step further, the location of possible sources of primary data may be specified in such *tertiary* sources as *Who's Who in Gerontology*, encyclopedias, dictionaries, and directories. Nondocumentary sources include formal and nonformal varieties. In the example above, the salesperson was a nonformal source, but the wall directory was a formal source. Personal contact with the original author or researcher may provide nonformal, nondocumentary information that in turn may also lead to the primary data.

Indexes such as the *Index to Periodical Literature on Aging* compile lists of references to primary data in journals. *The Handbook of Aging and the Social Sciences* selects essays written by authorities in the field and organizes the documents into a single volume.

Tertiary and nondocumentary sources basically guide the searcher to both secondary and primary sources of data. The *Directory of Gerontological Libraries and Information Centers* leads the information seeker to sources of documents or primary data. The Gerontological Society of America's publication *Who's Who*

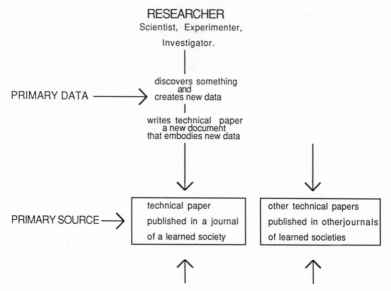

Secondary and tertiary sources are furnished to lead
the searcher back to these primary sources and
to other secondary sources.

Figure 6
Production of Documentary Sources

in Gerontology guides the user toward professionals in the field,
nondocumentary sources, who may in turn supply reprints of
primary data, secondary data sources such as bibliographies,
or his or her own research findings.

Entering the information sources can occur at many points.
Often the types of sources may overlap. Using the various resources depends on where you are at the moment, whether
you are new to the field of gerontology or a professional in the
field. The path to relevant information is not always a straight
line. If one is a novice, a handbook will provide not only an
overview of the topic, but a bibliography of primary sources,
and some indication of the authoritative authors in the field. If
you are a social worker in gerontology looking for information
that relates to health care, for example, you may look for an

Table 2

Production and Retrieval of Information

INFORMATION SOURCES	CHARACTERISTICS	DOCUMENTARY TYPES
Nondocumentary	Formal or nonformal sources of information leading to primary data or other resources	Formal: research organizations, professional associations, consultants Nonformal: discussions with colleagues or other professionals
Tertiary	Aids in using primary or secondary sources of information	Directories of organizations, guides to literature, handbooks, library collections, encyclopedias
Secondary	Organizes and repackages primary data to guide the researcher to the original	Bibliographies, indexes and abstracts, state-of-the-art literature, acquisition lists
Primary	Original reports of research and scientific investigation	Monographs, journal articles, conference reports, dissertations

← Production of
Information

index or abstract in the health-care area together with the associated gerontological resources.

Figure 5 shows how primary, secondary, and tertiary sources build on each other. Table 2 restates Figure 5 in tabular form to clarify how information is produced and how it is best retrieved. The table suggests that the most efficient retrieval of information is to reverse the process used in its production. The addition of the nondocumentary source in the chart, which is absent in Figure 5, suggests that such nondocumentary sources usually lie outside the formal structure of organization of the information itself. Such nonformal informants, when and where available, are sometimes the quickest aids to arriving at the desired information.

Often information source categories will overlap. A journal may be considered both a primary and secondary source of literature. Although it is a primary place of publication it also compiles and organizes previously published documents in a particular area of study. These documents are usually listed at the end of the individual author's paper. Many journals also include annual indexes to their previous volumes.

The importance of knowing the organization of literature sources is to expand one's knowledge of the available resource tools for answering the initial question.

To sum up: in order to bring together original or primary data and make it accessible to possible users, information is compiled into information resources that aid the researcher in sifting through the extensive wealth of material to locate the specific piece of information relevant to the researcher's topic or information needs. Original research produces primary data and is contained in primary sources, such as the journals of learned societies or their proceedings. References to it may then be incorporated into secondary sources such as indexes, abstracts, bibliographies, and computer databases that seek to coordinate information in specific subject areas. Guides to all such information resources are included in this volume.

4

HANDBOOKS, DIRECTORIES, AND ENCYCLOPEDIAS

In the previous chapter it was pointed out that the information on primary data is often organized and compiled into secondary sources such as handbooks, directories, and encyclopedias to help in its location. Because of the significance of secondary sources, particularly in the early stages of a search, as tools in locating information, they are listed in this chapter rather than in an appendix.

Handbooks are an extremely useful source of secondary information on the scientific and professional literature of a field of study. Although they may vary in format, they usually contain authoritative and technical summaries of all aspects of a discipline. Handbooks are an excellent source of information for both the professional and the novice.

The term *handbook* is used in a variety of ways. Many times a handbook is simply a guide on how to develop a program or a list of resource materials. This does not, however, reduce the usefulness of the text. The discussion in this chapter centers on handbooks that are a collection of essays or chapters written by specialists in gerontology or geriatrics. This type of handbook serves as an information tool for locating primary sources of data.

Handbooks, as discussed here, essentially show the various aspects and dimensions of a topic and thus provide an overview of key elements in a field of study. They may, as in *The Handbook of Mental Health and Aging,* include chapters by specialists in the field on the physiological, social, and economic as well as the psychological factors involved in mental health and older adults. An architect designing facilities for older adults, on the other hand, may need background information contained in a handbook on the physiological changes that occur with aging in order to design a structure in which handicapped individuals can function.

Handbooks can be valuable information resource tools for a preliminary search in gerontology or geriatrics. Through the use of a handbook, an individual who is a novice to gerontology or geriatrics can get an authoritative overview of the biology, psychology, or mental-health literature as it applies to aging. Because the essays or chapters are written by authorities, related documents on the specific topic can be retrieved by extending the search to a related index, abstract, or computer database, using the author of the essay or chapter as an entry point.

The terminology used in the handbooks provides subject terms that are appropriate to an ongoing search in such resources. Often subject terms will vary with different disciplines. An index in sociology, psychology, or the allied health fields will reflect the terminology used in that discipline. Correct terminology, as we said earlier, may be the key to locating relevant information sources.

In addition, handbooks often include extensive bibliographies that enable one to develop a preliminary bibliography on a more specialized topic. Using the *Social Sciences Citation Index* method of developing bibliographies, for example, the articles cited in the documents from the preliminary bibliographies included in the essays or chapters of a handbook often yield additional sources for a bibliography.

Figure 7 shows one method of conducting a preliminary search using handbooks as an information resource tool.

As shown in the figure, a handbook will furnish an overview of a selected topic, specify appropriate terminology, and provide bibliographic references. These can lead one in turn to three different, but related, ends—conducting an additional search for more authors in that area (in the case of an overview) is

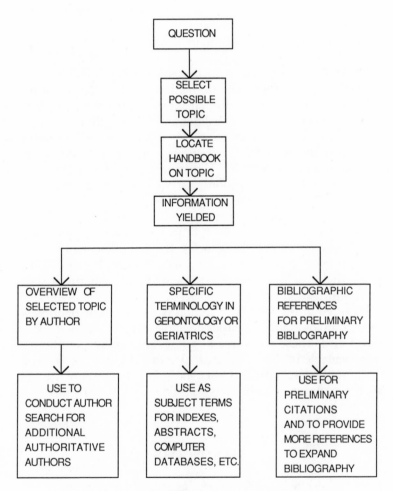

Figure 7
The Uses of Handbooks

only one option. The specific terminology retrieved can be used as subject terms in subsequent searches through indexes, abstracts, and computerized databases. That is a second option. The third option is to employ the retrieved bibliographic references not only for the construction of preliminary or expanded bibliographies, but as preliminary citations to the primary data that is being sought.

Directories are included in this section because they are a valuable source of tertiary information (see Chapter 3) supplying both formal and nonformal information resources. A research project on hospital facilities and services for older adults in the United States may require a directory to determine the types of facilities offered, the number presently available, and the location of the facilities. It may require additional information obtained from a telephone interview with an administrator in the facility. A directory may supply part or all of the information required above, depending on the type of directory used. Although directories are often difficult to locate, because many are developed by private agencies, there is a *Directory of Directories*, published annually in Detroit by the Gale Research Company, that is helpful in locating one that may be appropriate to your information needs.

Included in the following section is a list of basic handbooks in gerontology and geriatrics together with a selected list of directories. These will serve as guides to the types of information available in this area. Journals are not listed here but can be found in Appendix C. Other secondary and tertiary sources, such as indexes and abstracts, can be found in Appendix B.

HANDBOOKS

Bergener, Manfred, and Carl Eisdorfer, eds. *Psychogeriatrics: An International Handbook.* New York: Springer, 1986.

> Renowned scholars have contributed chapters on the current issues of psychogeriatrics. The problems of diagnosis and treatment are discussed, as well as the classification of specific disease processes and their treatment. It includes geriatric research

and its application to older adults in both private and institutional settings.

Binstock, Robert H., and Ethel Shanas, eds. *Handbook of Aging and the Social Sciences*. 2d ed. New York: Van Nostrand Reinhold, 1985.

The handbook focuses on aging and the social structures and social systems as they apply to the elderly. Knowledge of the aging process is presented from the perspective of a variety of social sciences, including anthropology, demography, economics, history and law as well as political science. The text organizes, evaluates, and explains research data, concepts, theories, and issues in aging from the social science viewpoint.

Birren, James E., and K. Warner Schaie, eds. *Handbook of the Psychology of Aging*. 2d ed. New York: Van Nostrand Reinhold, 1985.

This volume presents all aspects of the psychological development of the older adult. It covers the biological development and changes, the behavioral and social processes and the nervous system as well as learning, memory, sensory development, and personality theories. Psychiatric disorders, clinical assessment, treatment, and therapies are also included.

Birren, James E., and R. Bruce Sloane, eds. *Handbook of Mental Health and Aging*. Englewood Cliffs, N.J.: Prentice-Hall, 1980.

A wide spectrum of specialists review the relevant scientific and professional literature in the area of mental health and aging. Research has been collected from a wide range of scattered fields to provide a definitive reference source on all aspects of mental health and aging including the epidemiology of mental disorders, intelligence, problem solving, and the role of society and the family in mental health. Diagnosis and assessment, as well as treatment and prevention methods, are also presented.

Blumenthal, Herman T., ed. *Handbook of Diseases of Aging*. New York: Van Nostrand Reinhold, 1983.

The handbook is concerned with the pathogensis of a small group of disorders that account for almost all deaths from diseases in later life.

Breuer, Joseph. *Handbook of Assistive Devices for the Handicapped Elderly: A New Help for Independent Living*. New York: The Haworth Press, 1982.

The handbook acts as a reference guide for those in the physical and occupation therapy professions on the latest and most assistive devices for handicapped elders.

Busse, Ewald W., and Dan G. Blazer, eds. *Handbook of Geriatric Psychiatry*. New York: Van Nostrand Reinhold, 1980.

Contributors to the handbook include those in the field of psychiatry, biomedicine, and the behavioral sciences. The first ten chapters of the text are devoted to the biological and psychosocial bases of geriatric psychiatry. The second section is devoted to the diagnosis and treatment of disorders in later life.

Carstensen, Laura L., and Barry A. Edelstein, eds. *Handbook of Clinical Gerontology*. Elmsford, N.Y.: Pergamon Books, 1987.

This is a comprehensive multidisciplinary resource for researchers, practitioners, and students on the problems of aging. It focuses on health, pharmaceutical, social, and psychological factors. Sections on normal aging, psychological disorders, behavior management, medical issues, and social problems are presented.

Finch, Caleb E., and Edward L. Schneider, eds. *Handbook of the Biology of Aging*. 2d ed. New York: Van Nostrand Reinhold, 1985.

The revised edition of the handbook covers new areas pertinent to aging and gives new insights into the nervous, neuroendocrine, autonomic, heart, and cardiovascular systems. Other topics include physiology, the neurochemistry of aging, genetics, metabolism, and cell division.

Gambert, Steven R., ed. *Handbook of Geriatrics*. New York: Plenum, 1986.

A handbook of geriatric medicine that deals with the most prevalent illnesses among the aged, as well as illnesses that are atypical. It also includes a section on nutrition, selected neurological problems, and preventative health care for the aged.

Goldberg, P. B., and J. Roberts, eds. *CRC Handbook on Pharmacology of Aging*. Boca Raton, Fla.: CRC Press, 1983.

Contributions in the handbook are by pharmacologists who present the basic aspects of gerontological pharmacology.

Helgeson, Elisabeth M., and Scott C. Willis. *Handbook of Group Activities for Impaired Older Adults*. New York: The Haworth Press, 1987.

This volume offers practical information for conducting daily activities programs with severely impaired elders in a wide range of settings.

Holmes, Monica B., and Douglas Holmes, eds. *Handbook of Human Services for Older Persons.* New York: Human Sciences Press, 1979.

Hsu, Jeng M., and Robert L. Davis, eds. *Handbook of Geriatric Nutrition.* Park Ridge, N.J.: Noyes, 1981.

Articles are written by those experienced in the basic science and applied aspects of aging. The focus is on both the scientific principles and practical applications of nutrition and the aged.

Jenicke, Michael A. *Handbook of Geriatric Psychopharmacology.* Littleton, Mass.: PSG, 1985.

Killeffer, Eloise H. P., Ruth G. Bennett, and Gerta Gruen. *Handbook of Innovative Programs for the Impaired Elderly.* New York: Haworth Press, 1985.

A practical handbook for physical and occupational therapists that supplies an array of programs to meet the needs of elderly patients, including the severely debilitated.

Monk, Abraham, ed. *Handbook of Gerontological Services.* New York: Van Nostrand Reinhold, 1985.

The handbook provides practitioners with a comprehensive review of various types of social intervention methods and services available for the operation of new programs for the elderly today. It covers needs assessment, interventions, theories, and policies.

Palmore, Erdman B., ed. *International Handbook on Aging.* Westport, Conn.: Greenwood Press, 1980.

The text is an accumulation of information on the state of gerontology in a selected group of countries where significant work and development is taking place. A review of the history of gerontology accompanies each case. It includes an "International Directory of Organizations Concerned with Aging," "International and Regional Organizations on Aging," and the "International Development of Academic Gerontology." There are 89 tables of data on the aged.

Palmore, Erdman B., ed. *Handbook on the Aged in the United States.* Westport, Conn.: Greenwood Press, 1984.

Chapters include information on the demographic, psychological, and socioeconomic characteristics of various ethnic, religious, and special-problem groups. The editor covers the history, problems, and advantages in each group. A list of academic and research centers on aging are included as well as statistical tables on older Americans in general.

Poon, Leonard, ed. *The Handbook for Clinical Memory Assessment of Older Adults*. Washington, D.C.: American Psychological Association, 1987.

The handbook is concerned with the basic questions of memory dysfunction. It contains the latest research on the theoretical and clinical aspects of memory and includes tests and instruments for evaluation. The focus is on the anatomical, physiological, neurochemical, and genetic processes.

Schick, Frank L., ed. *Statistical Handbook on Aging Americans*. Phoenix, Ariz.: Oryx Press, 1986.

This volume provides recent statistical data about the aging population in the United States. Its contents cover the demographic, social, health, employment, and economic characteristics of the elderly. It also provides a guide to relevant information sources.

Steffl, Bernita, ed. *Handbook of Gerontological Nursing*. New York: Van Nostrand Reinhold, 1984.

Much of the content is organized around the role of the professional nurse as advocate, assessor, and intervener in the care of the older patient. The handbook includes basic information about nursing and aging, sensory deprivation, medical treatment, and the principles of rehabilitation of chronically ill elderly persons. The appendix offers a list of health-care resources, National Organizations and ANA standards of gerontological nursing practice and standards of care.

Sumner, E. D. *Handbook of Geriatric Drug Therapy for Health Care Professionals*. Philadelphia: Lea & Febiger, 1983.

The first section of the handbook is devoted to theories of aging, demographic trends, the psychosocial and psychological aspects of aging as well as pharmacokinetics. The second section provides information about drug dosage and special precautions for the elderly.

U.S. Department of Health and Human Services. Social Security Administration. *Social Security Handbook 1984.* Washington, D.C.: U.S. Government Printing Office, 1984.

The text includes a detailed explanation of the federal retirement, survivors, disability, supplementary security income programs, health insurance, and public assistance. It explains how these programs operate, who is entitled to benefits, and how these benefits can be obtained.

Watkins, Donald M. *Handbook of Nutrition, Health and Aging.* Park Ridge, N.J.: Noyes, 1983.

The handbook is intended to supply information to both those in the field of nutrition and those professionals who are nonmedical nutritionists but play a large role in delivering nutritional services to the aged.

Watson, R. R., ed. *Handbook of Nutrition in the Aged.* Boca Raton, Fla.: CRC Press, 1985.

There are four main sections in the handbook that include information on nutrition, disease, and body functions in the elderly. Other portions of the text cover vitamins and minerals, and specialized nutrition programs and therapies for the aged.

Wilson, L. B., S. P. Simson, and C. R. Baxter. *Handbook of Geriatric Emergency Care.* Baltimore: University Park Press, 1984.

The handbook is directed toward all practicing health-care providers. It fuses emergency medicine and geriatrics, and contains information on emergency medical disorders, psychiatric emergencies, nursing, and long-term care.

DIRECTORIES

American Association of Homes for the Aging. *Directory of Members.* Washington, D.C.: American Association of Homes for the Aging, annual.

A geographic directory that gives the name, address, and telephone number of the facility, and the name of the administrator. Information is also provided on sponsorship, levels of care, and services offered to nonresidents. It acts as a directory of homes for the aged as well as an information source for retirement communities and nursing homes in the United States.

Directory of Adult Day Care Centers. Washington, D.C.: U.S. Government Printing Office, 1980.

> The directory offers over six hundred day care programs and is arranged by states. Entries in the directory include the name and address, the sponsoring organization, the date the program started, and the nature of the program.

The Directory of Directories. Detroit, Mich.: Information Enterprises, 1988.

Directory of Hospital Services for Old Adults. Chicago: The Hospital Research and Education Trust, 1982.

> The directory is a state-by-state listing of hospital sources for older adults. It includes the name, address, and telephone number of the hospital, the types of service offered, and the name of the administrator.

Huff, Robert L., ed. *National Directory of Retirement Facilities.* Washington, D.C.: NRTA-AARP, 1979.

> A state-by-state directory of government subsidized housing for the elderly as well as private nonprofit housing. The name, address, and description of the facility is included.

Mongeau, Sam, ed. *Directory of Nursing Homes: A State by State Listing of Facilities and Services.* 2d ed. Phoenix, Ariz.: Oryx Press, 1984.

> The volume is arranged alphabetically by state and then by city. It lists the name, address, telephone number, levels of care provided, number of beds, and Medicaid, Medicare, or Medi-Cal certification. It also includes the name of the administrator; health services supervisor; ownership; staff members; special religious, recreational, and social activities; and admission requirements.

National Directory of Shared Housing Programs. Rev. ed. Philadelphia: Shared Housing Resource Center, 1983.

> Housing is listed according to state and city, with each listing identified as belonging to a special category such as a group residence or a match-up program.

Ownes, H. Jean. *Directory of Gerontological Libraries and Information Centers.* Detroit: University of Michigan–Wayne State University, Institute of Gerontology, 1980.

> The directory lists library and information centers by states, and includes the name, address, and telephone number together with a profile of the services available.

Raper, Ann Trueblood. *National Continuing Care Directory: Comprehensive Information on Retirement Facilities and Communities Offering Prepaid Contracts for Long-term Care (also called "Life Care").* Washington, D.C.: American Association of Retired Persons, 1984.

Descriptions of the life care communities are provided in the directory together with the location, admission requirements, charges for units, and services available.

U.N. International Directory of Organizations Concerned with the Aging. New York: U.N. Department of Economics and Social Affairs, 1977.

The directory contains information on 117 institutions in Africa, Asia, and Europe. It provides the names, addresses, and directors of the organizations as well as the objectives of each organization and the type of material published.

Who's Who in Gerontology. The Membership Directory of the Gerontological Society of America. Washington, D.C.: Gerontological Society of America.

The directory includes a worldwide list of members alphabetically by name and location, by discipline areas, and by geographical location.

ENCYCLOPEDIAS

Kruzas, Anthony T., ed. *Encyclopedia of Medical Organizations and Agencies.* Detroit: Gale Research, 1983.

This is a subject guide to medical societies, professional and voluntary associations, foundations, research institutes, governmental agencies, medical and allied health schools, information centers, database services, and related health-care organizations. It lists the name, address, telephone number, description, publications, computer-based products and services, research activities and fields, and state affiliates.

Maddox, George L., ed. *The Encyclopedia of Aging.* New York: Springer, 1987.

The encyclopedia features over five hundred entries of terms and concepts relating to the biomedical, psychological, and social aspects of aging. Explanations of terms and concepts are written by key authorities in the field of aging. The text is aimed at both researchers and students. One hundred and twenty-eight pages of references are provided as well as an index to more detailed subjects.

5

INDEXES AND
ABSTRACTS

Primary sources of information, especially journal articles or research reports, are often difficult and time consuming to locate. Although library card catalogs may list the names of periodicals in their collection, articles contained within them are not available through the card catalog. Because journals represent the most current research in a field they are the most sought-after documents. Indexing and abstracting services, aside from computerized database information systems, can be among the most efficient and quickest methods of locating both current information resources and retrospective data.

By definition, an index is a list. A mailing list may contain the names and addresses of all clients of a company. An index, such as one finds in the back of a book, is a list of all portions of the text that contain information on a particular topic. Bibliographies constitute lists of all reference sources on a selected topic or list all works of a particular author. Indexes and abstracts organize and list primary sources of information in a variety of disciplines, such as gerontology, psychology, and anthropology.

A published abstract is essentially an index, and in addition provides a brief description of the document, usually in one or two paragraphs. Often, the title of a document is insufficient in specifying its contents, and an abstract can determine whether or not the document is applicable to the topic at hand. By employing an abstract, the searcher can avoid the time and energy employed in tracking down a primary source document only to discover that the information it contains is not what is desired.

Some indexes may include annotations together with the citation, or some other brief notes commenting on the contents of a document. An annotation is simply a brief description of the material in one or two sentences. Brief notes, such as references to graphs, tables, or bibliographies, may be included with the citation in other indexes. Extra words, phrases, or short descriptions can be valuable aids for clarifying the relevancy of the material. A note on a four-page bibliography in an article directly related to a research question can be a "gold mine."

Some advantages of using an index are:

1. It provides the most current information on research.

2. It saves time browsing through journals.

3. It is useful for developing a bibliography.

4. It can provide historical or background coverage on a topic of research.

5. It can provide additional research documents by a specialist in a particular area.

6. It has the added advantage of locating missing information in a citation.

Because of the enormous amount of aging literature that is scattered throughout a wide range of disciplines, it is virtually impossible to compile all the data into one publication. An indexing service started in 1982 will rarely include earlier publications. It provides current information but lacks the historical data that may be necessary for its background. Because of these limitations on abstracting and indexing gerontology materials, it is often necessary to use indexing and abstracting publications from other disciplines. They provide additional information on a topic. Although the *Index to Periodical Literature on*

Aging will include articles on housing and the elderly, *The Architectural Index* will select more specialized documents relating to the structure and design of facilities for the aged.

All indexing and abstracting systems will contain the essential information for locating documents. This includes the complete citation to a book, journal article, or report and, in the case of abstracts, a summary of the document. They differ, however, in the scope of information indexed, its arrangement, and the type of document included in the index. The basic elements of the organization and scope of an index depend largely on the publisher.

The scope or coverage of the documents included in the index or abstract determines the kind of information retrieved. Each index differs, from the subject matter covered to the scope of the coverage. The *Index to Periodical Literature on Aging* selects journal articles primarily in social gerontology and the allied health fields. *Gerontological Abstracts* emphasizes the biological and clinical areas of aging with additional information on the social aspects. *Psychological Abstracts* covers information resources that include journal articles, books, or conference reports in the field of psychology and includes selected resources on the clinical research in psychology and aging. *Index Medicas* covers all information in the medical field including material in geriatrics. These resources will limit the documents included in the coverage to selections that meet their editorial criteria.

A specialist in the area of social work, psychology, or nursing is familiar with the information resources and tools in his or her area or field of speciality. Entering the information resources of other disciplines can present problems. The social worker may be familiar with resources in related disciplines such as psychology or sociology, but may be limited when it comes to economics or architecture. Knowing the type of information contained in an index reduces the amount of time and frustration involved in retrieving essential information. Appendix B contains a list of indexes and abstracts that contain information in gerontology and geriatrics. A brief explanation of each index and abstract is provided to explain the kinds of information included.

Because of the vast number of journals published today, indexes limit the materials they include to particular journals. Many of the index publications of other disciplines will index journals in gerontology or geriatrics that contain documents relative to the subject area. The *Journal of Housing for the Elderly*, for example, is indexed not only in *The Architectural Index* but also in *Public Affairs Information Bulletin (PAIS)* and *Social Work Research & Abstracts* and *Sociological Abstracts*. *ERIC–CIJE* selects articles from *Aging and Work, Educational Gerontology, The Gerontologist*, the *Journal of Gerontology*, and *The International Journal of Aging and Human Development* as well as from other appropriate journals in gerontology. Rather than using valuable time searching individual journals for articles, an index will provide the searcher with a cumulative listing of all articles on a topic from a variety of journals.

Selecting an index in other disciplines is initially determined by the scope of information contained in the index. A search for information on the design of housing for handicapped elderly may be located in *The Architectural Index*. The effect of the design of a housing environment on the psychological state of a handicapped elderly person, however, may be more appropriate to *Psychological Abstracts*. An index such as *ERIC–CIJE* will selectively include information in many of these areas, although it may not include in-depth coverage of the topic.

Table 3 shows selected examples of the types of subject area in both gerontology indexes and some of those of other disciplines.

An index may vary in the depth of the information selected. Although the publication *Gerontological Abstracts* contains articles on social gerontology, it also includes an extensive amount of data solely concerned with the physiological aspects of aging. A neurologist searching for information on changes in the structures of the brain in Alzheimer's patients will seek different types of information from the allied health professional or social worker. From a neurologist's standpoint, articles on the chemical factors and their effect on the brain or memory of an Alzheimer's patient may be significant, but this is not useful to the social worker explaining these effects to a client. The *Cumulative Index to Nursing & Allied Health Literature* may provide the extent and breadth of information needed by the social

Table 3
Subject Areas in Selected Indexes

Current Literature on Aging

Architectural barriers   Group homes
Care givers   Living arrangements
Dementia   Nursing homes
Elder abuse   Support systems

Gerontological Abstracts

Biochemistry   Psychology
Endocrinology   Learning and memory
Lymphoid system   Education
Central nervous system   Service delivery

Public Affairs Information Service Bulletin

Old age pensions   Health
Benefits   Housing
Care and treatment   Medical care
Economic conditions   Legislation

Business Periodicals Index

Elderly   Family relations
Day care   Housing
Economic conditions   Medical care
Employment   Elderly consumers

worker. Thus, the depth or complexity of the information is variable, and must be taken into account.

The arrangement of an index or abstract can often be a problem to the first-time user. Publishers of indexes and abstracts develop their own format for the arrangement of the material in the publication; however, all the essential information that allows the user to locate the document (author, title, journal, publisher, and date of publication) is included, although the arrangement of the information varies. Knowing what we may consider the common elements of all such indexes allows for greater versatility in locating the information one requires.

The *Social Sciences Citation Index* and its companion citation indexes contain the most comprehensive information resources; it is unlike any of the other indexes. Because the citation indexes are more complex and unique, it is essential to read the instructions provided in the front of the volume to insure the most efficient use of these indexes. Sample searches are included to help the user obtain the most information available from the indexes. A brief explanation of the *Social Sciences Citation Index* is provided in Appendix B.

Variations in the format of an index may range from a straight *A*-to-*Z* listing of the author, subject, and title in one volume, to separate sections for *author* and *subject* listings. An index that includes a subject and author section may only provide a code number in the author section referring the user to the subject section for complete information on documents.

Most indexes use some type of abbreviation for the citation. They may abbreviate the journal name, use a variety of formats for listing the volume and issue number and date; however, an explanation of the abbreviations is almost always provided in the book. Although most abbreviations can be easily "decoded" by the reader, the incorrect deciphering of the journal name can lead to problems. One such abbreviation in the *Cumulative Index to Nursing & Allied Health Literature* cites a journal as CLIN MANAGE PHYS THER. Is it "Physical Therapy" or "Physical Therapists"?

A publication of abstracts presents a wider range of variation in formating. Because of the amount of information presented on just one reference source, it is often more practical to list

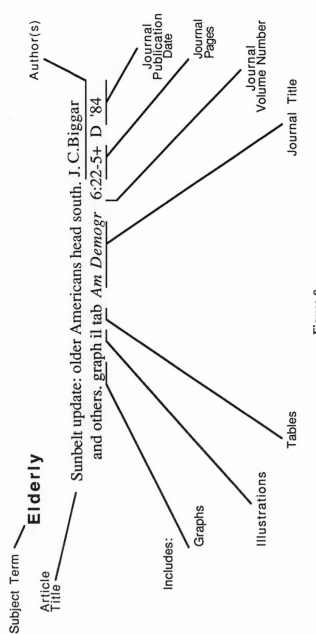

Figure 8
Sample Index Citation

Psychological Abstracts

Sample Abstract

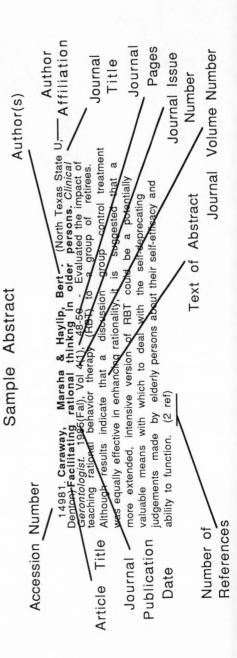

Accession Number

Author(s)

Author Affiliation

Journal Title

Journal Pages

Journal Issue Number

Journal Volume Number

Text of Abstract

Article Title

Journal Publication Date

Number of References

14981. **Caraway, Marsha & Haylip, Bert** (North Texas State U, Denton) **Facilitating rational thinkng in older persons.** *Clinical Gerontologist.* 1985(Fal), Vol 4(1), 48-59 - Evaluated the impact of teaching rational behavior therapy (RBT) to a group of retirees. Although results indicate that a discussion group control treatment was equally effective in enhancing rationality, it is suggested that a more extended, intensive version of RBT could be a potentially valuable means with which to deal with the self-deprecating judgements made by elderly persons about their self-efficacy and ability to function. (2 ref)

48

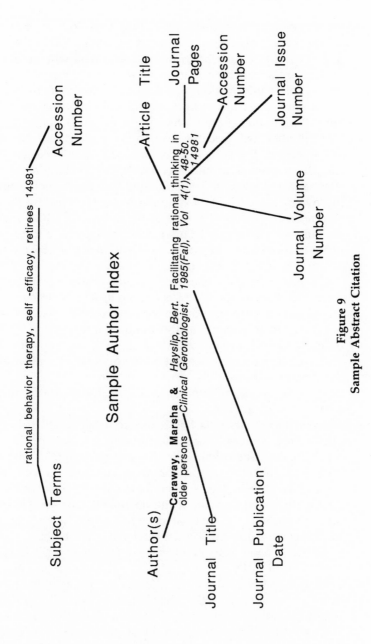

Figure 9
Sample Abstract Citation

49

the abstracts in a separate section together with an author or subject index, or simply a table of contents. The subject and title of an article may be in one section, while the author, location, and abstract are in another section. To lead the user to the complete information, a variety of coding systems is used. In the subject section of *ERIC–CIJE*, the title of the article and the full journal citation are listed. An *EJ* or *ED*, followed by a code number, will lead the user to the abstract and the name of the author. The subject index of *Sage Family Studies Abstracts* lists the subject term and a code symbol for locating the abstract and full citation. The following figures illustrate some of these variations. The first example is drawn from the *Business Periodicals Index* and is a sample of an index citation with its various parts identified. This index arranges its entries in alphabetical order by subject terms. One citation is broken down for the *Elderly* subject term (Figure 8).

The next example illustrates a sample abstract citation as included in *Psychological Abstracts* (Figure 9). The abstracts section includes all the information on the document plus an accession number. Other sections of the publication include a "Subject Index" and an "Author Index." Looking up the paper in either of these sections provides one with the accession number. In the abstracts section, the abstracts are in numerical order, so finding this accession number leads one directly to the abstract of the document.

Gerontological Abstracts has a different approach to locating information sources. The subject area is a "Table of Contents for Biological, Clinical or Social Aspects of Aging." Under each section are subheadings and only those subheadings with a page number contain abstracts. Included with the abstract are the author, title, and location of the document. The complete citation and abstract can be located by following the page number for the general subheadings in the table of contents.

Although *Social Work Research & Abstracts* has a "Field of Service" section in the opening pages of the volumes, it also has a subject section. Additional information on aging can be located in the subject section that is not included in the "Aging and the Aged Field of Service" section. The subject index provides the title of the article and the abstract number for locating the full information. It is best to consult both sections, because there is information in each section that is not in the other.

Despite the fact that indexes and abstracts may appear to be more confusing than they are worth, this is not the case. They often make it possible to locate documents that otherwise are obscure. A small amount of patience in learning to use a particular index is usually rewarded, no matter how obtuse it initially may appear. They each employ some basic scheme that can easily be decoded if one is patient and uses a detective's approach and looks for clues. Because complete information on the citation must be included in the volume, what is the code for locating it? Is there only one way of entering the index for locating the information, or are there several? If there are abbreviations present there must be a section that explains how to decode them. Despite variations in format and coding, there is always a system that allows you to "get there from here."

Indexes and abstracts are two of many information tools available. Although each has its own idiosyncracies, all information tools can lead us to what we are searching for. The initial research strategy discussed in Chapter 2 applies to all information tools. What is the question? Where is the answer? Handbooks and directories, as we saw in the last chapter, take a different approach. On-line databases take another (Chapter 7). The end results can be productive if the "mind" work is done ahead of time.

6

AGENCIES AND OTHER SPECIALIZED SOURCES

There is an enormous amount of information on aging available from agencies, clearinghouses, and organizations, although the quantity varies according to the types of information sought. Publications may be in the form of pamphlets, brochures, bibliographies on issues in aging, or various educational materials. Or it may consist of referrals to experts on specific topics. An agency or organization may, in turn, refer you to another information center that has more specific data related to your particular request.

Because the study of aging has reached far greater proportions in the past 10 or 20 years, many agencies that may at first appear to be unrelated to gerontology may now have materials on aging. With the increase of studies on the problems of alcohol abuse, for instance, the National Clearinghouse for Alcohol Information will now supply information on alcohol and aging.

Centers or agencies vary in the types of material offered as well as in the cost of their services. Some centers supply free information, while others charge a minimal fee. Information clearinghouses or centers will often supply a list of available products or services together with a price list of their available materials.

A list of agencies or centers in the United States supplying information is too extensive to compile here. However, the following list provides a sampling of the types of centers that supply information in gerontology and geriatrics. Perhaps the greatest advantage of such a listing is to make the reader aware of the extent of resources available. Quite often, contacting a central agency will lead to further resources in this area. The NRTA–AARP National Gerontology Resource Center, for example, will supply a list of nongovernment and federal agencies distributing aging-related materials.

The research strategy described in Chapter 2 is extremely useful when contacting an agency, whether by telephone or mail. The statement of your problem needs to be interpreted by another person, and the clearer the statement, the clearer the answer. Quite often the problem may simply be that you do not know what to specifically ask for. In that case, simply say so. The field is so differentiated that no one is expected to be familiar with all its parts.

The following is a list of agencies and organizations that supply information in the area of gerontology and geriatrics.

Administration on Aging
330 Independence Avenue, SW, Room 4146
Washington, D.C. 20201

American Aging Association (AGE)
42nd and Dewey Avenues
Omaha, Nebraska 68105

American Association of Homes for the Aging (AAHA)
1050 17th Street, NW, Suite 770
Washington, D.C. 20036

American Association of Retired Persons (AARP)
1909 K Street, NW
Washington, D.C. 20049

American Bar Association Commission on Legal Problems of the Elderly
1800 M Street, NW
Washington, D.C. 20036

American Foundation for the Blind
15 W. 16th Street
New York, New York 10019

American Geriatric Society
770 Lexington Avenue
New York, New York 10021

American Society for Geriatric Dentistry
2 N. Riverside Plaza, Suite 1741
Chicago, Illinois 60606

American Society on Aging
833 Market Street, Suite 516
San Francisco, California 94103

Association for Gerontology in Higher Education
600 Maryland Avenue, SW, West Wing 204
Washington, D.C. 20024

Food and Nutrition Information and Education Resources Center
National Agricultural Library Building
10301 Baltimore Boulevard
Beltsville, Maryland 20705

Gerontological Society of America (GSA) Information Service
1411 K Street, NW, Suite 300
Washington, D.C. 20005

Gray Panthers
3635 Chestnut Street
Philadelphia, Pennsylvania 19104

International Federation on Ageing (IFA)
1909 K Street, NW
Washington, D.C. 20049

Legal Research and Services for the Elderly
1511 K Street, NW
Washington, D.C. 20005

National Alliance of Senior Citizens
P. O. Box 28008
Washington, D.C. 20005

National Association of Area Agencies on Aging
600 Maryland Avenue, SW, West Wing 208
Washington, D.C. 20024

National Association of Nutrition and Aging Services Programs
1601 Second Avenue, Suite 800
Seattle, Washington 98104

National Association of State Units on Aging (NASUA)
600 Maryland Avenue, SW, West Wing 208
Washington, D.C. 20024

National Caucus and Center on Black Aged, Inc.
1424 K Street, NW, Suite 500
Washington, D.C. 20025

National Clearinghouse on Aging
300 Indepedence Avenue, SW
Washington, D.C 20201

National Clearinghouse for Alcohol Information (NCALI)
P. O. Box 2345
Rockville, Maryland 20853

National Clearinghouse for Mental Health Information
National Institute of Mental Health
5606 Fishers Lane
Rockville, Maryland 20857

National Clearinghouse of Technology and Aging
University Center on Aging
University of Massachusetts Medical Center
55 Lake Avenue
North Worcester, Massachusetts 01655

National Council of Senior Citizens
925 15th Street, NW
Washington, D.C. 20005

National Council of the Black Aged
P. O. Box 8813
Durham, North Carolina 27707

National Council on the Aging, Inc. (NCOA)
600 Maryland Avenue, SW, West Wing 100
Washington, D.C. 20024

National Geriatrics Society
212 W. Wisconsin Avenue
Milwaukee, Wisconsin 53203

National Gerontology Resource Center
1909 K Street, NW
Washington, D.C. 20049

National Health Information Clearinghouse
P. O. Box 1133
Washington, D.C. 20013

National Indian Council on Aging
P. O. Box 2088
Albuquerque, New Mexico 87103

National Information Center on Volunteerism
P. O. Box 4179
Boulder, Colorado 80306

National Institute on Aging Information Center
2209 Distribution Circle
Silver Springs, Maryland 20910

National Interfaith Council on Aging (NICA)
P. O. Box 11924
Athens, Georgia 30603

National Pacific–Asian Resource Center on Aging (NPARCA)
The Coleman Building, Suite 210
811 First Avenue
Seattle, Washington 98104

National Rehabilitation Information Center (NARIC)
The Catholic University of America
8th and Varnum Streets, NE
Washington, D.C. 20064

National Senior Citizens Law Center
1709 W. 8th Street
Los Angeles, California 90017

National Task Force on Drugs and the Elderly
Broome County Awareness Center
22 Park Place
Johnson City, New York 13790

National Urban League Advocacy for the Aged Project
55 E. 52nd Street
New York, New York 10022

Nutrition Information and Resource Center
Pennsylvania State University
University Park, Pennsylvania 16802

Older American Volunteer Programs (ACTION)
806 Connecticut Avenue, NW, Room 1006
Washington, D.C. 20025

Western Gerontological Society (WGS)
833 Market Street, Room 516
San Francisco, California 94103

Widowed Persons Service (AARP)
1909 K Street, NW
Washington, D.C. 20049

7

COMPUTERIZED INFORMATION RETRIEVAL SYSTEMS

An enormous and often overwhelming amount of information is available electronically today, including the on-line computer database Ageline developed by AARP specifically for gerontological information. This chapter provides a brief introduction to the techniques and resources useful for retrieving gerontology information on a variety of on-line databases. A selected list of computerized databases that contain information in gerontology and geriatrics is given in Appendix D.

The advent of microcomputers, or personal computers (PCs), has made on-line databases available not only to the large university library but to the neighborhood library as well. In addition, any person with a home computer may access these databases through conventional telephone services. If the computer or terminal does not contain a built-in telephone modem, these are now available in external configurations at reasonable cost. These devices connect the PC or terminal to the telephone lines via the conventional plug-in phone jack. The telephone is unplugged from the wall jack and plugged into the modem. Another jack on the modem accepts a plug from the computer and a line from the computer is then plugged into the wall jack.

The telephone may be used as before, but now the computer can also have access to the telephone lines. Instructions are furnished with the modem. A computer software program (such as BITCOM, MITE, or KERMIT) is then run at the computer. This allows one to dial the telephone number and to access the information service.

A distinction must be made between databases that contain the actual information and the services supplying them. An information service (such as DIALOG or COMPUSERVE) is an organization that provides telephone service users access to large numbers of specific databases, such as ERIC or Sociological Abstracts. Ageline, the gerontological database, can be accessed via BRS. Although these information services are located in various places throughout the country, and the databases as well, the user is provided with a local telephone number and the information service makes the long distance connections, at no charge to the user. There is a charge, however, for the use of each database, usually a function of the database used, the length of time it is used, and the time of day. Late hours are usually cheaper than the middle of the business day. Once a service has been accessed, the log-on procedure it employs to allow the user to scan specific databases varies, so the user should make some previous contact, either by mail or conventional voice telephone to the service and obtain whatever printed instructions are available relating to log-on procedures.

As in using any other information resource tool, it is important to know what types of information are available in particular databases, how to retrieve information electronically, and the methods of using computerized information systems. All the search strategies of Chapter 2 apply, but they are now applied via the computer.

Knowing where and what to look for in a database is similar to searching the library card catalog or using an index or abstracting system. The same information compiled in a printed index is stored in a computer as a database. Some databases have an equivalent printed index that contains much of the same information that is available on the database; however, the printed index may not be as current as the computerized database.

Printed indexes are available at most university libraries. Databases such as ERIC, PsychINFO, and Sociological Abstracts are a few that can be searched using a conventional printed index. The advantage of the computerized database is that the information is made available much earlier than its printed version, because printing and its distribution takes a much longer period of time.

In a library, or when using a printed copy of an index, you are able to scan the material to see what you do or do not want. If you do not use the correct terminology, there is a *see* or *see also* note to direct you to other subject terms. The computer database cannot make assumptions about what you are looking for, nor will it check to see if you are employing its terminology correctly. For example, if you enter the term *aged*, you may retrieve an enormous amount of information on aged trees or stones together with aged humans. If your terms do not match those in the database, you will not retrieve documents. It will not tell you to look elsewhere.

In searching an on-line database the same considerations employed in a manual search of the literature are equally, or perhaps even more, important. Understanding the problem or question to be answered, selecting appropriate subject terms, and selecting the information resources that contain information on your topic will enhance the results of the search. In fact, these are more important in electronic searching, because it is often incorrectly assumed that the computer knows all and does not make mistakes. This is in addition to the relatively high cost of on-line computer searching. It is important to keep in mind that the cost is a function of the time spent on-line; if excessive hunting for the correct combination of terms takes place, the resulting costs may be prohibitive.

Just as in using a printed index, the basic components of a search by author, title, or subject are available on-line. You may elect to search documents written by a key author on a selected topic, or use subject terms in general. As in a manual search, it is best to note the subject terms that best describe your topic, including both narrow and broad ones. Again, on-line "thinking" time is ticked off in dollars. A search query may retrieve five hundred documents on the subject or none at all. In either case you may have to change, add, or alter your terms. It may be necessary to consider whether or not the particular database uses the particular subject terms you entered. If there is a controlled vocabulary, it may be necessary to locate a database thesaurus, if one is available. Some databases, such as ERIC, allow "free text" or "natural language" searching. This allows the user to search for any word or phrase that appears in the titles and abstracts. In other words, you may search for particular words or combinations of words in the texts, and are not limited to subject terms.

Although Ageline and the printed index *Current Literature on Aging* will have all their information related to gerontology, on-line databases located in other disciplines require using a subject term in order to limit the search to the aged population. They may use the term *aged, elderly, older adults,* or *senior citizens.* In some cases you may want to combine and use two or more terms for the aged to ensure retrieving the most information.

Selecting an on-line database is similar to selecting a particular index or abstract. The *Cumulative Index to Nursing & Allied Health Literature* can be searched both manually and on-line for information on nursing and allied health information. If your topic is concerned with the planning and administration of health care you may choose to search the database Health Planning and Administration. Knowing the *kinds* of information contained in the database saves both time and money.

Many libraries offer computer search services; however, if you are conducting your own search on-line, you will need to be familiar with the procedures to access and search the information system. If you elect to use the DIALOG Information Services, Inc., which has an extremely large number of databases, it is a question of how to access DIALOG and the commands appropriate to the system. There are commands to get into the system, to select the database you want, and finally to carry out your search strategy. An extensive explanation is available in *How to Look It Up Online* by Alfred Glossbrenner. For information on all commercial and public sources of information, there is *The Computer Data and Database Source Book* by Matthew Lesko. Both are excellent examples of texts that can provide extensive information on the topic of on-line searching.

An important element in effectively searching on-line databases is an understanding of the concepts of Boolean algebra or set theory. This logic is graphically explained in the Venn diagrams of Figure 10. Perhaps the best explanation is given by McCormick in the text *The New York Times Guide to References Materials*. McCormick states (1986:32) that

> when one uses a computer, many search elements can be combined according to Boolean Logic. This system, invented by English mathematician George Boole (1815–1864), uses the connectors AND, OR, and NOT to link subject terms in ways that provide various combinations of the terms themselves: Boole's logic is different from the logic commonly assumed with these connecting words. For example, a searcher might assume that the AND connector equals "plus" and therefore that it adds terms together to make a greater sum (as in "I want cheese *and* crackers"). Also, it is usually assumed that the OR connector reduces the sum (as in "I want cheese *or* crackers but not both"). Actually, the opposite happens in Boolean Logic: AND reduces; OR expands.

The Venn diagrams (Figure 10) depict a search for information on the elderly and health services, narrowing the search to services for the black elderly. Using the OR connector, the search will retrieve *all* the documents on the elderly and *all* the documents on health services, including but not limited to those on the elderly. That is not what the searcher wishes; quite the contrary. When the terms are combined with the AND connector, however, the computer selects *only* those documents on the elderly that include information on health services as *they relate to the elderly*, thereby targeting the desired information and consequently *reducing* the total number of documents retrieved. If we go one step further and connect *elderly* AND *health services* AND *black*, we obtain *only* the documents relating to health services for the black elderly. The number of documents is reduced further. This process (known technically as a "reduction of property space") targets the desired information exactly. This is a key strategy in computerized searching. An in-

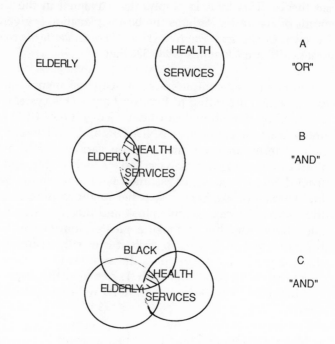

Figure 10
Venn Diagram of a Boolean Search

(A) The "OR" operation yields ALL documents relating to the elderly and ALL documents relating to health services. (B) The "AND" operation yields ONLY those documents relating to health services for the elderly. (C) The "AND" operation on these three terms yields ONLY those documents relating to health services for black elderly.

formation retrieval system such as DIALOG informs you, as you search, of the number of documents your search terms have retrieved. By progressively narrowing down the scope of the subject one arrives at the specific documentary sources desired, if they are there. The diagrams do not show the use of the NOT connector. The NOT connector simply allows the searcher to eliminate any unwanted subject areas. If *health care* AND *elderly* NOT *whites* is searched, the system retrieves documents relating to the health care of elderly nonwhites; this would include Orientals, native Americans, blacks, etc. and would obviously produce a separate, but related group of documents to that produced in the previous example.

Just as there are limitations in indexes and abstracts, there are limitations in on-line databases. The scope of material included in a database may be limited to selected journals. Documents may be included by the editors according to how they relate to a particular discipline. However, although the database ERIC is considered an educational database, its selection criteria allow it to include a wide range of gerontology journals and it therefore includes a great deal of information on the health, social, psychological, and economic aspects of aging. This is not true of most databases.

On-line databases may not locate retrospective or historical information. They may include documents from 1975 or 1980 to the present, for example, depending on the date the database was developed. If the database is more recent, it may be wise to check the period it covers. There are also language limitations. International databases will include documents in languages other than English, in which case you may need to limit the retrieval of documents by specifying a particular language. You may retrieve vital documents; however, they may be in Finnish.

The greatest advantage of on-line database searching is the speed in which you can retrieve the most up-to-date information. An enormous amount of material can be searched in an extremely short period of time. An added advantage, especially in a multidisciplinary area such as gerontology, is the ability to switch from one discipline's publications to another by simply switching databases. If Sociological Abstracts does not have what you want, you may immediately select to search PsychINFO or ERIC. Many databases will provide abstracts of articles or the full text of an article and information can be printed on-line or off-line. Off-line costs are lower. It may be best to print only a few citations on-line, to check for relevancy, and then request off-line printing of the others. Off-line retrieval involves requesting copies of the citations while you are still on-line. Printed copies of the citations and/or abstracts are then forwarded to you through the mail.

Just as other information resources may vary in their arrangement and scope, on-line databases also vary. There is the additional problem of cost for services. The hourly fee is often a key consideration in determining the selection of a database. There is also the question of whether a computerized search is always more appropriate than a manual search. A relatively simple search is best conducted manually; however, where the question involves multiple concepts, or spans two or more disciplines, a computer search is more comprehensive and less time-consuming.

REFERENCES

Glossbrenner, Alfred. *How to Look It Up Online*. New York: St. Martin's Press, 1987.

Lesko, Matthew. *The Computer Data and Database Source Book*. New York: Avon Books, 1984.

McCormick, Mona. *The New York Times: A Guide to Reference Materials*. Rev. ed. New York: New American Library, 1986.

The above books contain a great deal of information on information retrieval systems and databases and can form the core of a small library in this area. For specific information on on-line information services, contact the following services.

ON-LINE INFORMATION SERVICES

BRS Information Technologies
1200 Route 7
Latham, New York 12110

COMPUSERVE
    5000 Arlington Centre Boulevard
    Columbus, Ohio 43220
DIALOG Information Services, Inc.
    3460 Hillview Avenue
    Palo Alto, California 94304

8

COMMUNITY RESOURCES

In searching for information on the elderly it is sometimes necessary to enquire into their situation in a local community. The information resource tools for the local level vary from region to region, from state to state. Nevertheless, a wealth of information is available from national and state sources that relate directly to the local community, and these are often supplemented by publications produced by local agencies (see Chapter 6) and official and regional interest groups. Although the data in these sources may not be broken down directly into elderly or aging categories, there is often a breakdown by age, date of birth, residence, and the like. These data may be the only information available on local elderly. They will include nursing-care facilities, retirement homes, Meals On Wheels locations, and the names and addresses of organizations serving the elderly, for example.

The material that follows can serve as a model for information resources at the local community level. In this case, a medium-size city, Syracuse, located in Onondaga County in the center of New York State, provides the exemplary materials. Other medium-size and larger cities can be expected to have similar and perhaps greater information resources that include references to organizations, services, and officials related to the aged in their communities. The information searcher should attempt to duplicate these kind of sources and the kind of publications shown here as they may be applicable to the particular community about which gerontological information is sought.

DEMOGRAPHIC AND STATISTICAL INFORMATION

Congressional Information Service. *American Statistics Index: A Comprehensive Guide to the Statistical Publications of the United States Government.* Washington, D.C.: Congressional Information Service, 1973–, annual.

Consists of a base edition with monthly and annual supplements, issued in two parts: index and abstracts. The index is arranged by subject; index entry leads to data description in the abstracts volume. Publications may be located and retrieved through information provided in the abstracts.

Rand McNally 1983 Commercial Atlas and Marketing Guide. Chicago: Rand McNally, 1983.

Provides statistical coverage and authoritative interpretation of business data. Includes current economic and geographic information for the United States and Canada by region and metropolitan area, and general statistical information about the world.

U.S. Bureau of the Census. *Block Data.* Bureau of the Census, Washington, D.C.

Statistics from the 1980 Census of Population and Housing, by block on the general characteristics of housing units and population. Block statistics were collected for urbanized areas, incorporated places of 10,000 or more inhabitants outside of these urban areas, and areas choosing to participate in the Bureau's contract block statistics program.

U.S. Bureau of the Census. *Block Statistics, United States Summary.* Bureau of the Census, Washington, D.C.

U.S. Bureau of the Census. *County and City Data Book.* Prepared by the Social and Economic Statistics Administration, Bureau of the Census, Washington, D.C.

Contains statistical data for each county in the United States, over three hundred Standard Metropolitan Statistical Areas

(SMSA) and over eight hundred cities of 25,000 or more inhabitants. Presents sample data on education, the labor force, income, etc. and includes information on other topics such as nursing homes, Medicare, bond ratings, and heating and cooling days.

U.S. Bureau of the Census. *Current Population Reports*. Bureau of the Census, Washington, D.C.

Produced intermittently by the Bureau of the Census, in series form. Covers a variety of topics, including population estimates and projections, statistical profiles, and trends in social and economic conditions.

U.S. Bureau of the Census. *Directory of Federal Statistics for Local Areas*. Bureau of the Census, Washington, D.C.

A guide to local socioeconomic data contained in publications of 33 federal agencies for local areas. Provides table-by-table descriptions of statistical reports on areas smaller than states. Arranged alphabetically by subject of report.

U.S. Bureau of the Census. *Small Area Statistical Papers*. Bureau of the Census, Washington, D.C.

The methodology and use of small-area statistics in decision making are given as well as the 1977 economic census and its use in private and public sectors. Includes how to find data in small areas.

U.S. Bureau of the Census. *Statistical Abstract of the United States*. Prepared by the Social and Economic Statistics Administration, Bureau of the Census, Washington, D.C., 1978–, annual.

A standard summary of statistics on social, political, and economic organization of the United States. Designed to serve as a statistical reference and a guide to other statistical publications and sources. Includes introductory text to each section, source notes for tables, a Guide to Sources of Statistics, and a Guide to State Statistical Abstracts. Topics include population, health and nutrition, education, law, employment, income, energy, and housing.

U.S. Bureau of the Census. *United States Census Reports*. Bureau of the Census, Washington, D.C.

Provides data in the form of tables on a variety of subjects such as mobility and migration, education, fertility, income, and economy. The introduction to each volume covers background, related information, explanations, and comparisons.

DIRECTORIES AND INDEXES

Bryfogle, Charles R., ed. *City in Print: An Urban Studies Bibliography.* Ontario, Canada: Learning Press, 1974.

Available at the Onondaga County Public Library.

A Checklist of Official Publications of the State of New York. Albany: University of the State of New York, State Education Department, 1947–, monthly.

The contents include excerpts of governor's remarks, statistical analyses, lists of departments and materials available, addresses of agencies, etc.

Dictionary Catalog of Official Publications of the State of New York. Albany: University of the State of New York, State Education Department, quarterly.

The dictionary includes all New York State monographs cataloged at the New York State Library, in Albany. All entries are interfiled in alphabetical order. Published in quarterly, cumulative issues with an annual cumulative edition and five-year cumulations.

Index to Current Urban Documents. Westport, Conn.: Greenwood Press, 1972–, quarterly.

Indexes a majority of the known local documents issued annually by the 264 largest U.S. cities, including Syracuse. Onondaga County Public Library has the microfische collection.

U.S. Library of Congress. *Monthly Checklist of State Publications.* Library of Congress, Division of Documents, Washington, D.C, 1910–, monthly.

Records state documents received by the Library of Congress. Includes some city and county materials, monographs, periodicals, publications of organizations and associations, and statistical reports. Arranged by state and issuing agency.

LOCAL GOVERNMENT ASSOCIATIONS

Association of Town Clerks, Onondaga County

Onondaga County Association of Mayors and Village Officials

Onondaga County Supervisors Association

NEW YORK STATE INFORMATION

NYNEX Yellow Pages and White Pages for Syracuse Metropolitan Area, NYNEX Information Resources.

The directory lists all city departments and names of department heads as well as some employees and their telephone extensions.

Bureau of HMO and Home Health Services
Office of Health Systems Management
Empire State Plaza Tower Building, Room 1970
Albany, New York

Information on health care.

League of Women Voters of the Syracuse Metropolitan Area. *Patterns of Government in Onondaga County, New York: Structure and Services of County, City, Town and Village Governments.* Syracuse, New York, 1970.

A guide to understanding the basic structures and functions of local government. Part one covers the history and structure of local government in Onondaga County, including finances and political. Part two describes services provided by local government.

League of Women Voters of New York State. *New York State: A Citizen's Handbook.* New York, 1964.

Explains in layman's terms how a bill becomes a law, the structure of state courts, systems for voter registration, organization of political parties, etc. Includes information on the constitution, executive departments, administrative departments, and local government.

MacRae's New York State Industrial Directory. New York: MacRae's Blue Book, Inc., 1985–.

Manufacturers are listed by county, with company name and corporate affiliation, address, telephone number, product description, plant and property size, etc. An "Index to Counties and Municipalities" identifies the towns within the counties listed. Updated annually.

The New York Red Book. Albany, N.Y.: Williams Press, 1892–, annual.

An informal presentation of pertinent facts regarding New York State, its political subdivisions, and the officials who administer its affairs. Recognized and accepted as a source of reliable information by public officials, news agencies, and the general public. Contains biographies of all members of the state legislature, judges, and executive officials. Available free to state residents from their state senator.

N.Y. State Division of the Budget. *New York State Statistical Yearbook.* Prepared by the Office of Statistical Coordination, State Division of the Budget, Albany, New York, 1986.

Data on New York State provided by nearly 60 public organizations. Includes names, locations, and activities of state agencies, and statistics on population, health and human services, education, employment and income, banking, agriculture, transportation, and natural resources.

Polk's Syracuse (Onondaga County), New York, City Directory.

Published annually. Includes a descriptive section with statistical review, historical sketch, etc. Yellow pages provide a classified listing of business and professional concerns, a list of residents, businesses and professional affiliations, marital status, occupation, and address of each adult resident. (See also *Polk's Syracuse Suburban City Directory,* covering suburban areas within a 30 mile radius of the city.)

Syracuse Onondaga County Planning Agency. *Syracuse and Onondaga County Fact Book.* Prepared by Information Services Section, Syracuse Onondaga County Planning Agency, Syracuse, New York, 1979.

Contains county demographics and information about commerce, transportation, utilities, taxes, local government, employment, income, and community resources. It consolidates a wide variety of data, facilitates information retrieval, and presents a detailed summary of area resources.

SAMPLES OF SPECIALIZED INFORMATION SOURCES

Bureau of Municipal Research
City Hall, Room 215
Syracuse, New York 13202

Chamber of Commerce
1 Syracuse Square
Syracuse, New York 13202

The publications provided mainly include business and industrial directories, city and county statistics, real estate listings, maps, recreation information, current and projected financial trends, and business organizations.

Croner, Helga, ed. *National Directory of Private Social Agencies.* New York.

Provides listings of about 15,000 agencies, homes, and organizations that give direct help to individuals, and organizations that refer individuals to appropriate sources of help. Loose-leaf, 1964, monthly.

Erie Canal Museum Library
Canal Museum
Erie Boulevard East
Syracuse, New York 13202

Kruzas, Anthony Thomas, ed. *Social Service Organizations and Agencies Directory.* Detroit: Gale Research, 1982.

Gives a subject approach to national associations and state and local government agencies providing funding, coordination, and information that enable the social service system to function on a nationwide basis. Describes organizations and provides addresses and telephone numbers. Name and key word index.

U.S. Department of Commerce, Office of Telecommunications. *Geographical Areas Serviced by Bell and Independent Telephone Companies in the United States.* Washington, D.C.

APPENDIX A

GENERAL READING LIST ON AGING

AGING—PERSPECTIVES

Ardito, Stephanie, and Marta Dosa. *Gerontological Information: Conceptual and Historical Background*. Encyclopedia of Library and Information Science, v. 36 (187–219). New York: Marcel Dekker, 1983.

The article is an extensive in-depth study of the historical development of gerontology as a field of study, and the development of information resources related to this field. The authors show the growth of information services on all levels from the researcher to services for disseminating information to older persons. Coverage of the topic includes the characteristics of gerontological information, the issues and problems of dissemination, as well as the bibliographic control and problems associated with a multidisciplinary field. It also contains an excellent bibliography of 135 references on the topic.

Atchley, Robert C. *Social Forces and Aging*. 4th ed. Belmont, Calif.: Wadsworth, 1985.

Formerly titled *The Social Forces in Later Life*, the newest edition has changed its focus, organization, content, and format. The text is more interdisciplinary and includes information on legislation, demography, economics, and political issues.

Blau, Zena S. *Old Age in a Changing Society*. New York: New Viewpoints, 1973.

The author presents a realistic assessment of changes that occur following widowhood and retirement, and includes methods to prepare the individual to cope with these changes.

Busse, Ewald, and George L. Maddox. *The Duke University Longitudinal Studies on Normal Aging, 1955–1980: An Overview of History, Design, and Findings*. New York: Springer, 1985.

The authors present an overview of the studies and findings on the biological, behavioral, and social aspects of aging.

Cowgill, Donald O. *Aging Around the World*. Belmont, Calif.: Wadsworth, 1986.

The commonalities and varieties of aging experiences are shown through value systems, kinship and family roles, economic and political systems, and education.

Freeman, Joseph T. *Aging: Its History and Literature*. New York: Human Sciences Press, 1979.

The text provides the most comprehensive and systemic bibliography of the history and documentation of the vital themes in aging.

Hendricks, Jon, and C. Davis Hendricks, eds. *Dimensions of Aging*. Cambridge, Mass.: Winthrop, 1979.

A compilation of papers on the historical, cultural, social, psychological, and physiological aspects of the aging process.

Hendricks, Jon, and C. Davis Hendricks, eds. *Aging in Mass Society: Myths and Realities*. 3d ed. Boston: Little, Brown & Co., 1986.

The text illustrates the complexities of growing old and includes topics that deal with ageism and the common stereotypes that effect the elderly.

Krout, J. A. *The Aged in Rural America: An Annotated Bibliography of Social Service Research*. Westport, Conn.: Greenwood Press, 1986.

The bibliography is a comprehensive review of the existing social science publications on America's rural elderly. Included in the bibliography are journal articles, books, government publications as well as conference proceedings.

Louis, Harris, and Associates. *Myth and Reality of Aging.* Washington, D.C.: National Council on the Aged, 1975.

> The survey represents an extensive study of the public's attitudes toward aging and examines America's perception of being old.

Palmore, Erdman. *Normal Aging I. Reports from the Duke Longitudinal Study, 1955–1969.* Durham, N.C.: Duke University Press, 1970.

Palmore, Erdman. *Normal Aging II. Reports from the Duke Longitudinal Studies, 1970–1973.* Durham, N.C.: Duke University Press, 1974.

> The two volumes of *Normal Aging* represent a report on the Duke Longitudinal Studies that cover areas such as health, intelligence, family, social issues, and aging. The objectives and methodology of the study are included.

Quadagno, Jill S. *Aging in Early Industrial Society: Work, Family, and Social Policy in Nineteenth Century England.* New York: Academic Press, 1982.

> The impact of social change on the aged is explored through the analysis of historical records from nineteenth-century England.

Schaie, K. Warner, ed. *Annual Review of Gerontology and Geriatrics.* Vol. 7. New York: Springer, 1987.

> The present volume of the *Review* is concerned with research in geriatric psychophysiology.

Stearns, Peter N., ed. *Old Age in Preindustrial Society.* New York: Holmes and Meier, 1982.

> The social and political arrangements of older persons in societies from the Renaissance through the nineteenth century are explored primarily from the view of the historian and anthropologist.

ADULT EDUCATION

Glendenning, F., ed. *Educational Gerontology: International Perspectives.* New York: St. Martin's Press, 1985.

> Chapters in the text draw on educational developments and experiences in Europe and the United States. It covers areas in gerontological education and education of the older adult.

Long, Huey B. *Adult Learning: Research and Practice*. New York: Cambridge University Press, 1983.

The author addresses the special teaching and learning characteristics of the older adult and the nature of the educative process for this age group.

Lowy, Louis. *Education and the Later Years*. Lexington, Mass.: Lexington Books, 1984.

An investigation of the developmental, psychological, and social factors involved in educating the elderly are the focus of the text.

Peterson, Richard E., and Associates. *Lifelong Learning in America*. San Francisco: Jossey-Bass, 1980.

The purpose of the text is to provide a program-planning perspective for those hoping to implement education for mature learners.

ALZHEIMER'S DISEASE

Dobrof, Rose. *Social Work and Alzheimer's Disease: Practical Issues with Victims and Their Families*. New York: Haworth Press, 1986.

New and innovative social work roles with Alzheimer's disease clients and their families in hospital and nonhospital settings are covered in the text.

Kelly, William, ed. *Alzheimer's Disease and Related Disorders: Research and Management*. Springfield, Ill.: Charles C. Thomas, 1984.

The book covers the treatment of Alzheimer's disease and related disorders including research, practice, and policy. Descriptions are given of the neurobiological and neuropathological aspects of the disease.

Reisberg, Barry, ed. *Alzheimer's Disease: The Standard Reference*. New York: Free Press, 1983.

Covered in the text are areas such as the history and background of Alzheimer's disease, the pathological aspects, as well as diagnostic procedures and psychotherapeutic treatment.

ARTS AND ACTIVITIES

Bright, Ruth. *Music in Geriatric Care.* 2d ed. Sherman Oaks, Calif.: Alfred, 1985.

Music as a means of therapy with older persons is explored. The author also includes guidelines and ideas for establishing programs in nursing homes and geriatric units in hospitals.

Cusack, Odean, and Elaine Smith. *Pets and the Elderly: The Therapeutic Bond.* New York: Haworth Press, 1984.

An in-depth exploration of the use of pets as adjuncts to traditional therapy with the elderly is discussed. Structural and procedural suggestions and techniques for implementing programs are included.

Greenblatt, Fred S. *Drama with the Elderly: Acting at Eighty.* Springfield, Ill.: Charles C. Thomas, 1985.

The importance of drama for older adults is examined together with practical programs and advice on the use of drama to encourage creative expression.

Lerman, Liz. *Teaching Dance to Senior Adults.* Springfield, Ill.: Charles C. Thomas, 1984.

Provided in the text are techniques for teaching dance to older adults for both personal and public performances. It includes exercises as well as the therapeutic aspects of dance.

McGuire, Francis A., ed. *Computer Technology and the Aged: Implications and Applications for Activity Programs.* New York: Haworth Press, 1986.

Essays in the text provide information on the uses and advantages of computers in activities involving the aged.

McPherson, Barry D., ed. *Sport and Aging.* Champaign, Ill.: Human Kinetics, 1986.

The contributors explore the benefits and techniques for developing sports for older persons.

Weisberg, Naida, and Rosilyn Wilder, eds. *Creative Arts with Older Adults: A Sourcebook.* New York: Human Sciences Press, 1985.

Creative art leaders and therapists present experiences and theories related to working with older adults in nursing homes, community centers, and psychiatric institutions.

DEATH AND DYING

Blues, Ann G., and Joyce V. Zerwekh. *Hospice and Palliative Nursing Care*. Orlando, Fla.: Grune and Stratton, 1984.

The text covers a broad spectrum of information concerning the comprehensive care of dying persons and their family members.

Buckingham, Robert W. *The Complete Hospice Guide*. New York: Harper & Row, 1983.

The Guide presents the fundamentals of hospice care, the needs of the dying, and methods of implementing the hospice concept.

Corr, Charles A., and Donna M. Corr, eds. *Hospice Care: Principles and Practice*. New York: Springer, 1983.

The text provides information on hospice principles and practice, and the type of care essential to dying persons.

Kalish, Richard A. *Death, Grief, and Caring Relationships*. 2d ed. Monterey, Calif.: Brooks-Cole, 1985.

The process of dying together with the causes and stages, fear and anxiety, and caring relationships are covered by the author.

Kalish, Richard, and David K. Reynolds. *Death and Ethnicity: A Psychocultural Study*. Farmingdale, N.Y.: Baywood, 1981.

The authors present the various attitudes and reactions to death within different cultural groups.

Kastenbaum, Robert, and Ruth B. Aisenberg. *The Psychology of Death*. New York: Springer, 1972.

A synthesis of what is known and foreseen about man's changing relationship to death is the focus of the book.

Kubler-Ross, Elisabeth. *On Death and Dying*. New York: Macmillan, 1969.

Using interviews with dying patients as illustrations, the author focuses on the emotional stages in the process of dying.

Miller, Marv. *Suicide after Sixty*. New York: Springer, 1979.

This research study analyzes the issues concerned with suicide and the elderly, and the factors that contribute to the elderly's weakened coping abilities.

Munley, Anne. *The Hospice Alternative: A New Context for Death and Dying.* New York: Basic Books, 1983.

The hospice movement is discussed in relation to contemporary American society. The appendix includes hospice program standards and a state directory of hospice organizations.

Parkes, C. M. *Bereavement: Studies of Grief in Adult Life.* New York: International Universities Press, 1972.

The focus of the text is on the physical and mental consequences of bereavement.

DEMOGRAPHICS

Aging America Trends and Projections 1985–86. Prepared by the U.S. Senate Special Committee on Aging in conjunction with the American Association of Retired Persons, the Federal Council on the Aging, and the Administration on Aging. U.S. Department of Health and Human Services, Washington, D.C., 1986.

Rosenwaike, I., and B. Logue. *The Extreme Aged in America.* Westport, Conn.: Greenwood Press, 1985.

The focus of the data is on those 85 years and older. The text covers sex, age, race, ethnic groups, living arrangements, health, and implications for national policy.

Schick, Frank L., ed. *Statistical Handbook on Aging Americans.* Phoenix, Ariz.: Oryx Press, 1986.

The text includes current statistical data on the demographic, social, health, and economic status of the elderly. Most data are in tabular form.

U.S. Bureau of the Census. America in Transition: An Aging Society. *Current Population Reports,* special studies, ser. P-23, no. 128. Prepared by Cynthia M. Tauber. Washington, D.C., 1983.

Included in the text are facts on demographic, social, and economic conditions of older adults, as well as tables, charts, and graphs on numerical growth, income, health status, and other social characteristics.

Williams, Blanch S. Characteristics of the Black Elderly, 1980. *Statistical Reports on Older Americans,* no. 5. Washington, D.C.: National Clearinghouse on Aging, 1980.

Statistical tables and analysis of the marital status, household composition, labor force, income and poverty as well as education, health, and life expectancy are covered in the text.

Zopf, Paul E., Jr. *America's Older Population.* Houston, Tex.: Cap and Gown Press, 1986.

Using demographic data from the 1980s on, the author presents statistical data on older persons by age and sex composition, marriage and family status, education, work, retirement, and income. He examines the characteristics of the population and does a comparative analysis by sex, race, ethnicity, and location.

DEVELOPMENTAL DISABILITIES

Janicki, Matthew, and Henryk M. Wisniewski. *Aging and Developmental Disabilities: Issues and Approaches.* Baltimore, Md.: Paul H. Brookes, 1985.

The authors integrate current information in gerontology together with data on the developmentally disabled, presenting information in areas such as epidemiological studies, genetic aspects of aging, as well as needs and services for this group.

ECONOMICS

Estes, Carroll, et al. *Political Economy, Health and Aging.* Waltham, Mass.: Little, Brown & Co., 1984.

The authors view the interrelationship between polity, economy, and society, showing how the socioeconomic structure is responsible for the policies that alienate the elderly from society.

Schulz, James H. *The Economics of Aging.* 4th ed. Dover, Mass.: Auburn House, 1988.

An analysis is presented of all the major aspects of aging in America. It addresses both individual and social policy issues that affect the economic life of the elderly.

FAMILY RELATIONSHIPS

Bengston, Vern L., and Joan F. Robertson, eds. *Grandparenthood*. Beverly Hills, Calif.: Sage, 1985.

The major research themes on grandparenthood are reviewed showing the various perspectives on grandparenting.

Brubaker, Timothy H. *Later Life Families*. Beverly Hills, Calif.: Sage, 1985.

An examination is made of the research on later life families relating to marital status, support systems, widowhood, and the divorced and never married. Practice and policy implications are included.

Kingson, Eric R., Barbara A. Hirshorn, and John M. Cornman. *Ties That Bind: The Interdependence of Generations*. Washington, D.C.: Seven Locks Press, 1986.

The authors trace the key elements in the approach to intergenerational relationships in the latter quarter-century in America.

Shanas, Ethel, and Gordon F. Streib, eds. *Social Structure and the Family*. Englewood Cliffs, N.J.: Prentice-Hall, 1965.

Shanas, Ethel, and Marvin B. Sussman, eds. *Family, Bureaucracy, and the Elderly*. Durham, N.C.: Duke University Press, 1977.

The papers in this collection relate to how family networks and the aged deal with the bureaucratic structures.

Troll, Lillian, S. Miller, and R. C. Atchley. *Families in Later Life*. Belmont, Calif.: Wadsworth, 1979.

The authors stress the variations in family structures that exist in the United States today and the implications for counseling and psychotherapy.

GERIATRICS

Abrahams, Joel P., and Valerie J. Crooks. *Geriatric Mental Health*. New York: Grune & Stratton, 1984.

Divided into four sections, the authors provide an overview of knowledge in this area, including information on depression, dementia, and therapeutic techniques as well as social policies and ethics.

Andres, Reubin, Edwin L. Bier, and William R. Hazzard. *Principles of Geriatric Medicine*. New York: McGraw-Hill, 1985.

Designed for the medical practitioner, the book presents those aspects of geriatric medicine that are essential to the care of older persons.

Bray, J., and S. Wright, eds. *The Use of Technology in the Care of the Elderly and the Disabled*. Westport, Conn.: Greenwood Press, 1980.

The major papers and conclusions from the Commission of the European Communities relating to technology and the care of the aged and disabled are assembled in the text.

Cassel, Christine K., and John R. Walsh. *Geriatric Medicine*. Vols. I and II. New York: Springer-Verlag, 1984.

Volume I covers the medical, psychiatric, and pharmacological aspects of geriatrics, whereas Volume II focuses on the fundamentals of patient care.

Lederman, Ellen. *Community Resources for Geriatric Programs: A Practical Guide*. Springfield, Ill.: Charles C. Thomas, 1985.

The guide presents methods of finding and using community resource programs that can enhance the life of the elderly.

Rossman, Isadore, ed. *Clinical Geriatrics*. 3d ed. Philadelphia: J. B. Lippincott, 1986.

This enlarged edition contains new chapters on age-related immunologic alterations and on the digestive tract. The text is useful for primary care physicians.

Thompson, M. K. *The Care of the Elderly in General Practice*. New York: Churchill Livingston, 1984.

The milieu of care as well as the psychosocial problems confronting geriatric patients is the focus of the text.

Wood, W. G., and R. Strong, eds. *Geriatric Clinical Pharmacology*. New York: Raven Press, 1987.

The papers in the text focus on factors affecting drug response in the elderly individual, compliance, infectious diseases, and the immune function.

HEALTH

Brody, Elaine M. *Mental and Physical Health Practices of Older People: A Guide for Health Professionals.* New York: Springer, 1985.

A study of health practices of older people is used as data to describe the methodology, characteristics, and findings. Case histories are included together with health education training materials.

Kart, Cary S., Eileen S. Metress, and James F. Metress. *Aging and Health: Biologic and Social Perspectives.* Menlo Park, Calif.: Addison-Wesley, 1978.

The text presents a broad view of aging and health and includes areas relating to institutionalization, death and dying, and professional responsibilities in geriatric care.

Rowe, John W., and Richard W. Besdine, eds. *Health and Disease in Old Age.* Boston: Little, Brown & Co., 1982.

Each section of the text includes the normal physiology of aging and the related changes due to aging and disease.

HOUSING AND THE ENVIRONMENT

American Institute of Architects. *Design for Aging: An Architect's Guide.* Washington, D.C.: American Institute of Architects, 1986.

A guide developed to aid professionals in the field in designing facilities for the elderly.

Chellis, Roberto D., James F. Seagle, and Barbara M. Seagle. *Congregate Housing for Older People: A Solution for the 1980's.* Lexington, Mass.: Lexington Books, 1982.

Distinguished architects, psychologists, physicians, and managers discuss the needs and problems of elderly housing and the implications for a supportive environment for older adults.

Golant, Stephen M. *A Place to Grow Old: The Meaning of Environment in Old Age.* New York: Columbia University Press, 1986.

Based on interviews with older residents, the authors investigate the influence of residential environments on older citizens.

Koncelik, Joseph A. *Aging and the Product Environment.* Stroudsburg, Penn.: Dowden, Hutchinson and Ross, 1982.

Both products and design of equipment for the elderly are discussed in relation to the physiological changes due to the aging process. Drawings and charts are included.

Lawton, M. Powell. *Environment and Aging.* 2d ed. New York: Center for the Study of Aging, 1986.

The theoretical and applied issues in the design of the elderly environment are covered, together with the human behavioral system and social policy implications.

Newcomer, Robert J., M. P. Lawton, and T. O. Byerts, eds. *Housing an Aging Society: Issues, Alternatives and Policy.* New York: Van Nostrand Reinhold, 1986.

The book is intended to sensitize those working in the area of housing and the elderly to the needs of the aged and their families. Information is included on the varieties of housing available, the relationship of housing to the care of the elderly, as well as public and policy issues.

Raschko, Bettyann B. *Housing Interiors for the Disabled and Elderly.* New York: Van Nostrand Reinhold, 1982.

The text is concerned with interior design from the viewpoint of architecture, rehabilitation technology, product design, and environmental and behavioral literature.

Streib, Gordon F., Edward Folts, and Mary Anne Hilker. *Old Homes— New Families: Shared Living for the Elderly.* New York: Columbia University Press, 1984.

The research focuses on shared living arrangements for older people, the multiplicity of these arrangements, and the sociological understanding of this phenomenon.

LAW

Grimes, Richard. *Law and the Elderly.* Dover, N.H.: Croom Helm, 1985.

Discussed in the text are the personal and financial problems that face the elderly, in areas such as housing, social security, health care, and the family.

Kapp, Marshall B., and Arthur Bigot. *Geriatrics and the Law: Patient Rights and Professional Responsibilities.* New York: Springer, 1985.

The text is a general guide to the legal issues of the care of geriatric patients. It covers issues such as informed consent, involuntary commitment, legal services to the aged, and medico-legal issues in nursing homes and at death.

LONG-TERM CARE

Brody, Elaine M. *Long-Term Care of Older People: A Practical Guide.* New York: Human Sciences Press, 1977.

The focus of the text is on the services needed to enhance the care and treatment of long-term care clients in a variety of settings.

Eustis, N., J. Greenberg, and S. Patten. *Long-Term Care for Older Persons: A Policy Perspective.* Monterey, Calif.: Brooks Cole, 1984.

Using a multidisciplinary approach, the authors examine the issues of long-term care for the at-risk population relating to nursing home care and noninstitutional services. Policy development and reform are also examined.

Getzel, George S., and M. Joanna Mellor, eds. *Gerontological Social Work Practice in Long-Term Care.* New York: Haworth Press, 1983.

Contributions from practitioners and academics cover both the direct practice issues and theoretical approaches in long-term care of the elderly.

Harrington, Charlene, R. J. Newcomer, and C. L. Estes and Associates. *Long Term Care of the Elderly: Public Policy Issues.* Beverly Hills, Calif.: Sage, 1985.

An overview is given of the political, social, and economic issues of long-term care, including the states' responses to federal policy changes. Elements of an adequate long-term care system are also included.

Zawadski, Rick T., ed. *Community-Based Systems of Long-Term Care.* New York: Haworth Press, 1984.

Essential information for the planning of long-term care services is included in the text. Case studies are used to describe noninstitutional long-term care service models.

MINORITY AND ETHNIC ISSUES

Cohen, Elias S. *Minority Aged in America.* Ann Arbor, Mich.: University of Michigan–Wayne State University, The Institute of Gerontology, 1971.

An exploration is made of the problems and needs of the black and native American aged.

Dancy, Joseph. *The Black Elderly: A Guide for Practitioners.* Ann Arbor: Mich.: The University of Michigan–Wayne State University, The Institute of Gerontology, 1977.

The strengths, needs and problems of the black elderly are explored as well as their heritage and traditions.

Davis, Lenwood G. *The Black Aged in the United States: An Annotated Bibliography.* Westport, Conn.: Greenwood Press, 1980.

The bibliography lists and describes books, articles, dissertations, theses, and government publications devoted to the vital issues concerning the black aged.

Gelfand, Donald E. *Aging: The Ethnic Factor.* Boston: Little, Brown & Co., 1982.

An interdisciplinary approach is taken to the ethnic variables in the aging process and the methods various ethnic groups employ to deal with the problems. Issues covered focus on the resources, needs, and support systems of the ethnic aged.

Gelfand, Donald E., and A. J. Kutzik, eds. *Ethnicity and Aging: Theory, Research and Policy.* New York: Springer, 1979.

A compilation of essays that cover a wide range of problems and research dealing with ethnic groups.

Jackson, Jacquelyn J. *Minorities and Aging.* Belmont, Calif.: Wadsworth, 1980.

The author presents an overview of the issues related to minority aging and includes the biological, psychological, and social issues involved. It includes an extensive bibliography.

Momeni, Jamshid A. *Demography of Racial and Ethnic Minorities in the United States: An Annotated Bibliography with a Review Essay.* Westport, Conn.: Greenwood Press, 1984.

Murguia, Edward, et al. *Ethnicity and Aging: A Bibliography*. San Antonio, Tex.: Trinity University Press, 1984.

> The bibliography covers books, journal articles, and conference proceedings concerning blacks, Hispanics, native Americans, and Asian and Pacific Americans.

NURSING HOMES

Bowker, L. H. *Humanizing Institutions for the Aged*. Lexington, Mass.: Lexington Books, 1982.

> The text investigates humanization strategies in institutions for the elderly, and makes comparisons among geriatric institutions.

Johnson, Colleen L., and Leslie A. Grant. *The Nursing Home in American Society*. Baltimore, Md.: The Johns Hopkins University Press, 1986.

> The authors focus on nursing homes as a sociocultural phenomenon in American society and address issues concerning the care of nursing home patients.

U.S. Institute of Medicine. Committee on Nursing Home Regulation. *Improving the Quality of Care in Nursing Homes*. Washington, D.C.: National Academy Press, 1986.

> The study presents recommendations for the improvement of nursing homes, and includes a state-of-the-art appraisal as well as a history of Federal Nursing Home regulations.

NUTRITION

Dunkle, Ruth, Grace J. Petot, and Amasa B. Ford. *Foods, Drugs and Aging*. New York: Springer, 1986.

> The authors cover issues in nutrition, pharmacology, and aging in relation to areas such as nutrient interrelationships affecting the elderly, chemotherapy, polypharmacy, and treatment.

Feldman, Elaine B. *Nutrition in the Middle and Later Years*. New York: Warner Books, 1986.

The author presents the behavioral as well as the biochemical aspects of eating as it relates to the population of those 45 years and older.

Natow, Annette B., and Jo-Ann Heslin. *Geriatric Nutrition*. Boston: CBI, 1980.

This work provides an exhaustive review of the literature, and focuses on issues such as alcohol and caffeine, drug and food interaction, and dietary supplements.

Rockstein, Morris, and Marvin L. Sussman, eds. *Nutrition, Longevity, and Aging*. New York: Academic Press, 1976.

An overview is given of the essential biological changes in later life including the biochemical effects of nutrition, metabolism, vitamins, and care of the elderly with special diseases.

PHYSIOLOGY

Goldman, R. and M. Rockstein, eds. *Physiology and Pathology of Human Aging*. New York: Academic Press, 1975.

The proceedings of a symposium focusing on both the normal and pathological processes of aging.

Rockstein, M. *Biology of Aging*. Belmont, Calif.: Wadsworth, 1979.

The major theories of aging, structural and functional changes, and the pathology of aging are covered in the text.

Timiras, P. S. *Developmental Physiology and Aging*. New York: Macmillan, 1972.

A comprehensive text that covers all aspects of physiological changes over the life span, from fertility to adulthood, and the adult years to senescence.

PSYCHOLOGY

Botwinick, Jack. *Aging and Behavior: A Comprehensive Integration of Research Findings*. 3d ed. New York: Springer, 1984.

A comprehensive text on the psychological aspects of aging that includes areas such as personality and cognition, learning, biological and environmental issues, and decision-making processes.

Botwinick, Jack, and M. Storandt. *Memory, Related Functions and Age.* Springfield, Ill.: Charles C. Thomas, 1974.

The report focuses on the many different kinds of memory, clinical tests of brain function and brain damage, tests of psychomotor speed and intelligence, and personality and health.

Bromley, D.B. *The Psychology of Human Ageing.* 2d ed. Baltimore, Md.: Penguin Books, 1974.

The text covers both the biological and social aspects of aging, as well as mental illness and the psychopathology of older adults.

Eisdorfer, Carl, and D. Cohen. *Mental Health Care of the Aging.* New York: Springer, 1982.

Current treatment strategies are explored in the field of geriatric psychiatry using both pharmacological and psychotherapeutic methods.

Eisdorfer, Carl, and M. Powell Lawton, eds. *The Psychology of Adult Development and Aging.* Washington, D.C.: American Psychological Association, 1973.

The text summarizes the state of psychological knowledge about aging and includes essays by noted authorities on a wide range of topics.

Kaufman, Sharon R. *The Ageless Self: Sources of Meaning in Later Life.* Madison, Wis.: University of Wisconsin Press, 1986.

Themes, values, and structural meanings are used to demonstrate the relationship between cultural patterns and individual elderly lives.

Kermis, Marguerite D. *The Psychology of Human Aging: Theory, Research and Practice.* Boston: Allyn & Bacon, 1984.

The factors that affect aging are covered in such areas as the sensory and psychomotor processes, cognitive processes, personality and adjustment, and psychiatric disorders.

Marshall, Victor, ed. *Later Life: The Social Psychology of Aging.* Beverly Hills, Calif.: Sage, 1986.

Neugarten, Bernice L., et al. *Personality in Middle and Later Life.* New York: Atherton Press, 1964.

The authors explore the various approaches to the psychological study of aging and the personality.

Schaie, K. Warner, ed. *Longitudinal Studies of Adult Psychological Development.* New York: Guilford Press, 1983.

Seven of the major longitudinal studies of adult psychology are included in the text. It addresses the methodological issues involved and the empirical findings.

Zarit, Steven H. *Aging and Mental Disorders.* New York: Free Press, 1980.

The author surveys the biological, psychological, and social aspects of mental disorders and aging, and discusses assessment and diagnosis in the care of the elderly.

RETIREMENT

Atchley, Robert C. *The Sociology of Retirement.* New York: John Wiley & Sons, 1976.

Focus of the text is on the evolution of retirement as a product of industrial society.

Geist, Harold. *The Psychological Aspects of Retirement.* Springfield, Ill.: Charles C. Thomas, 1968.

The problems of retirement are examined, including the physiological and psychological effects that occur within individuals.

Miletich, J. J. *Retirement: An Annotated Bibliography.* Westport, Conn.: Greenwood Press, 1986.

The bibliography covers a wide range of topics including physical and psychological health, finances, housing and transportation, and work after retirement.

Osgood, Nancy J., ed. *Life After Work: Retirement, Leisure, Recreation and the Elderly.* New York: Praeger, 1982.

Contributors present an in-depth analysis of the institutions of work and leisure in the United States, an overview of the emerging institution of retirement and an examination of the relationships between work experiences and retirement experiences.

Palmore, Erdman B., et al. *Retirement: Causes and Consequences.* New York: Springer, 1985.

The text features a statistical analysis of the causes and consequences of retirement and explores a variety of socioeconomic groups that include those partially retired and those in forced retirement.

RESEARCH

Kane, Rosalie A., and Robert L. Kane. *Assessing the Elderly: A Practical Guide to Measurement.* Lexington, Mass.: Lexington Books, 1981.

The text provides explanations, evaluations, and comparisons of the most common measurement tools used to evaluate the physical, mental, and social functioning of clients. It analyzes the functions, strengths and limitations of each type of measurement tool.

Mangen, David J., and Warren A. Peterson, eds. *Research Instruments in Social Gerontology.* Vols. 1–3. Minneapolis, Minn.: University of Minnesota Press, 1982–1984.

This group of volumes compile, describe, and evaluate research instruments in gerontology. The first volume covers clinical and social psychology, while the remaining volumes include the research instruments and measurements.

Riley, Matilda White, B. B. Hess, and K. Bond, eds. *Aging in Society: Selected Review of Recent Research.* Hillsdale, N.J.: Erlbaum Associates, 1983.

Contributors to the collection present historical perspectives as well as current perspectives of scientific research on the psychosocial issues of aging.

SEXUALITY

Burnside, Irene M., ed. *Sexuality and Aging.* Los Angeles: The University of Southern California Press, 1975.

The publication is a product of multidisciplinary efforts by biologists, physicians, social psychologists, nurses, and social workers to present a complete compilation of information on sexuality and aging.

Butler, Robert N., and Myrna Lewis. *Love and Sex after 60*. New York: Harper & Row, 1986.

The authors propose a means for countering negative attitudes toward older persons and sexuality that appear in the culture. Common medical and emotional problems are discussed together with normal physical changes.

Walz, Thomas, and Nancie S. Blum. *Sexual Health in Later Life*. Lexington, Mass.: Lexington Books, 1987.

The authors study the role of sexuality in the health of older adults and discuss the effects of chronic illness, medical treatment, and drugs on sexuality. They also consider sexuality in institutional environments.

Weg, Ruth B. *Sexuality in the Later Years: Roles and Behavior*. New York: Academic Press, 1983.

The text explores sex roles and behavior, and discusses the possibilities for sexual fulfillment against a backdrop of negative societal attitudes.

Wharton, G. F. *Sexuality and Aging: An Annotated Bibliography*. 2d ed. Metuchin, N.J.: Scarecrow Press, 1981.

The bibliography represents an extremely comprehensive listing of references on all aspects of sexuality and aging.

SOCIAL POLICIES AND ISSUES

Browne, W., and L. K. Olson. *Aging and Public Policy: The Politics of Growing Old in America*. Westport, Conn.: Greenwood Press, 1983.

The main focus of the book is on the influence of macroeconomic conditions that shape public policy and the aged. The authors examine the role of interest groups, policy makers, and the elderly themselves in influencing policy.

Lammers, William W. *State Policies and the Aging: Sources, Trends and Options*. Lexington, Mass.: Lexington Books, 1984.

The text examines the sources of state policies, as well as changing trends and future plans. Topics covered include health and long-term care, income, and social services.

Lowy, L. *Social Policies and Programs on Aging.* Lexington, Mass.: Lexington Books, 1980.

A comprehensive look at the implications of social, economic, health, housing, and social service policies on the aged.

Myles, John. *Old Age in the Welfare State: The Political Economy of Public Pensions.* Boston: Little, Brown & Co., 1984.

Using an historical approach, the author studies the public pension systems in capitalist democracies. Cross-national differences and variations in pensions are examined.

Woodruff, Diana S., and James E. Birren. *Aging: Scientific Perspectives and Social Issues.* 2d ed. Monterey, Calif.: Brooks Cole, 1983.

Representing a current perspective on aging, the authors examine the aging process, its problems and the services and needs essential to the elderly.

SOCIAL PROBLEMS

Adelman, R. C., and D. Klitz, eds. *Alcoholism and Aging: Current Advances in Research.* Boca Raton, Fla.: CRC Press, 1982.

Contributors to the text cover the major areas of research concerned with alcoholism and aging.

Alston, Letitia T. *Crime and Older Americans.* Springfield, Ill.: Charles C. Thomas, 1986.

An examination is made of the victimization of the elderly, the causes and consequences of fear, the older offender, and the future of crime and the older population.

Costa, Joseph J. *Abuse of the Elderly: A Guide to Resources and Services.* Lexington, Mass.: Lexington Books, 1984.

The author combines chapters on elder abuse and crimes against the elderly with a directory of programs, advocacy groups, and other organizations that serve the abused elderly. The text includes a list of training materials.

Levin, J., and W. C. Levin. *Ageism: Prejudice and Discrimination Against the Elderly.* Belmont, Calif.: Wadsworth, 1980.

Lopata, H. Z., and H. P. Brehm. *Widows and Dependent Wives: From Social Problem to Federal Programs.* New York: Praeger, 1986.

The focus of the text is on the effect of the Social Security Act on the social provisions and the economic dependency of women and children in U.S. society.

Maddox, George, Lee N. Robins, and Nathan Rosenberg, eds. *Nature and Extent of Alcohol Problems among the Elderly.* New York: Springer, 1985.

Data from longitudinal studies on the nature and extent of alcohol problems are used to examine the psychological and social correlates of different age groups.

Quinn, Mary Joy, and Susan K. Tomita. *Elder Abuse and Neglect: Causations, Diagnosis, and Intervention Strategies.* New York: Springer, 1986.

The authors explore the phenomenon of elder abuse and neglect, and provide guidelines for detection as well as methods of intervention.

Yin, Peter. *Victimization and the Aged.* Springfield, Ill.: Charles C. Thomas, 1985.

An overview of crimes affecting the elderly is the focus of the text, including areas such as rape, robbery, assault, and burglary. Recommendations for action at the neighborhood and social level are provided.

SOCIAL SECURITY

Achenbaum, W. Andrew. *Social Security: Visions and Revisions.* New York: Cambridge University Press, 1986.

The history of social security from the New Deal to the Reagan era is covered, and guidelines for future policy is discussed.

Gaumnitz, Jack E., and Erwin A. Gaumnitz. *The Social Security Book.* New York: Arco, 1984.

The text covers general background information on the Social Security system, including its concepts, benefits, and programs. Changes in the 1983 law are included.

SOCIOLOGY

Bengston, V. L. *The Social Psychology of Aging.* New York: Bobbs-Merrill, 1973.

In a study of three generations of a single family the author demonstrates aging as a function of time and the social process.

Borgatta, F., and M. McCluskey, eds. *Aging and Society.* Beverly Hills, Calif.: Sage, 1980.

Against the background of profound demographic changes in the aging population, a dozen leaders in the field analyze key issues in the social and behavioral sciences.

Clark, M. M., and B. G. Anderson. *Culture and Aging.* Springfield, Ill.: Charles C. Thomas, 1967.

The authors present a sociocultural perspective on the problems of aging in the United States for a variety of cultural groups.

Cummings, E., and W. E. Henry. *Growing Old: The Process of Disengagement.* New York: Basic Books, 1961.

The theory of disengagement from life activities is presented as a psychosocial phenomenon.

George, L. K. *Role Transitions in Later Life.* Belmont, Calif.: Wadsworth, 1980.

The author focuses on stress, personal and social resources, coping processes and criteria of social adjustment among the elderly.

Harris, O., and W. Cole. *The Sociology of Aging.* Boston: Houghton Mifflin, 1980.

The authors examine social institutions, religion, cultural values and socialization as it applies to aging.

Rosow, Irving. *Socialization to Old Age.* Berkeley: University of California Press, 1975.

The focus of the text is on the development of norms and roles in the socialization of older adults.

Shanas, Ethel, ed. *Aging in Contemporary Society.* Beverly Hills, Calif.: Sage, 1970.

Contributors to the text discuss the various issues and problems of aging in present day society.

WOMEN

Coyle, Jean M. *Women and Aging: A Selected Annotated Bibliography.* Westport, Conn.: Greenwood Press, 1988.

References in the bibliography include books, films, dissertations, government documents, and journal articles related to the aging process. Subject areas include sexuality, religion, economics, and racial and ethnic groups as well as international issues.

Haug, Marie R., A. B. Ford, and M. Sheafor, eds. *The Physical and Mental Health of Aged Women.* New York: Springer, 1985.

The text focuses on the special health and social needs of older women. Issues related to institutionalization, health-care delivery, and epidemiological profiles of older women are also included.

Lesnoff-Caravaglia, Gari, ed. *The World of the Older Woman.* New York: Human Sciences Press, 1985.

Contributors to the book discuss the psychosocial problems of older women, including abuse, rape, and widowhood.

Markson, Elizabeth W. *Older Women: Issues and Prospects.* Lexington, Mass.: Lexington Books, 1983.

The author examines the various aspects of older women's lives and the problems unique to them. Issues relate to areas such as appearance, sexuality, employment, family relationships, and risk factors.

APPENDIX B

SELECTED LIST OF INDEXES AND ABSTRACTS

The following list of indexes and abstracts includes those in gerontology and geriatrics, as well as those in other disciplines that include information on aging. Key index and abstracting services have been selected to provide additional sources of aging information in other major disciplines. Because each index or abstract has its own unique arrangement and coverage, a brief description of the index is provided.

Abstracts in Anthropology. Farmingdale, N.Y.: Baywood.

> The publication consists of a two-volume group of eight issues each 12-month period. Each issue has a cumulative subject index. The table of contents groups information into main subject areas; however, there is also a subject and author index included in each issue. The subject index provides a code number for locating the abstract and citation. The abstract is primarily useful for information on the cultural and physical anthropology of aging.

The Architectural Index. Ervin J. Bell, ed. Boulder, Colo.: The Architectural Index.

> Published yearly, the index is useful for information on the design and structure of facilities for the elderly. References are arranged under subject headings with geographical subheadings.

Arts & Humanities Citation Index. Philadelphia: Institute for Scientific Information.

> This index uses the same format for arrangement of material as the *Social Sciences Citation Index*. The "Permuterm Subject Index" uses every significant word in the title of a current article and is paired with other significant words that appear in the title. Information can be retrieved using the terms *aged* and *elderly*, as well as other terms related to aging. Complete bibliographic descriptions of articles can be found in the "Source Index."

Business Periodicals Index. New York: H. W. Wilson.

> Except for August, the index is published monthly with a yearly cumulation. Coverage is provided for all aspects of business and includes information on the economic and financial aspects of aging in areas such as social security, retirement, employment of older workers, nursing homes, and longevity. All information is arranged alphabetically by subject, with information on aging under the term *elderly* with appropriate subheadings.

Cumulative Index to Nursing & Allied Health Literature. Glendale, Calif.: Cumulative Index to Nursing & Allied Health Literature.

> The index is published six times a year and includes journals and serials, pamphlets, and U.S. government publications on national legislation regarding basic health plans. The arrangement is alphabetical by subject and author in separate sections. Information on aging includes treatment and care of the elderly in a variety of settings. Subject terms tend to be more specific, relating to *geriatrics, longevity,* and *Alzheimer's disease*. Information can be retrieved using the terms *aged* or *aging*. Although there are no annotations, a citation may include reference to documents such as survey, research, or statistics.

Current Index to Journals in Education (ERIC–CIJE). New York: Macmillan.

> Although this is titled "Index" it is also an abstracting service. *Education* is used in a very broad sense and includes information on the social and psychological aspects of aging as well as educational gerontology. Published monthly, each issue contains a separate subject and author index, with a separate section for abstracts. Most of the information on aging is listed under the term *older adults*. The subject index provides the title of the document and the journal citation. *CIJE* uses an *ED* or *EJ*

plus a numerical coding system for locating the full citation and abstract. *ERIC–CIJE* also indexes unpublished documents that are available on microfische.

Current Literature on Aging. Washington, D.C.: National Council on the Aging.

The index is a quarterly guide to selected books and journal articles. The first three issues of the index are limited to a subject index whereas the last issue has a cumulative author and subject index with a code number referring to the complete citation and abstract. Core journals in gerontology are indexed in their entirety, while articles from other related fields are selectively indexed for gerontology related information.

Gerontological Abstracts. Ann Arbor, Mich.: University Information Services.

Published six times a year in two volumes, the index covers all aspects of the journal literature in gerontology with emphasis on the biological, clinical, and social aspects of aging. The table of contents acts as a subject index under the headings "Biological," "Clinical," and "Social Aspects." The main subject areas of the table of contents are subdivided into more specific areas such as, "Biological—Biochemistry," "Cell Biology," and "Endocrinology." Only those subheadings with page numbers contain abstracts and citations to articles.

Gerontology and Geriatrics. Amsterdam, The Netherlands: Excerpta Medica.

An international index that deals primarily with topics in the physiological field of aging, experimental gerontology, and articles related to institutional topics such as hospitalization and nursing, rehabilitation, or social welfare. Published ten times a year, each issue contains an abstract section and a subject and author index. Information is cumulated annually. The front of the index has a listing of broad terms that may be used to enter the general literature of, for example, psychology or nutrition. The subject index uses each keyword from the title of the document as a subject term. Using the terms *aged* or *elderly* will limit articles to those on aging. Following the key words in the article is a numerical code for locating the complete citation and abstract.

Hospital Literature Index. Chicago, Ill.: American Hospital Association.

The scope of the index is on the administration, planning, and financing of hospital and related health-care institutions. Information on the elderly is primarily concerned with the hospital environment and health-care delivery services. Each issue of the index contains an author and subject index. Although the subject term *aged* is used, other terms such as *geriatric care* or *geriatric nursing* are used to locate information on the aged.

Human and Animal Aging. Philadephia: Biosciences Information Service.

This abstract is a small subset of abstracts from *Biological Abstracts* that includes information and experimental studies on the clinical, biological, and psychological aspects of aging in both animals and humans. It is published twelve times a year. Because it has no index, it is primarily worthwhile for browsing for current research.

Human Resources Abstracts: An International Information Service. Beverly Hills, Calif.: Sage.

The index is published four times a year with a cumulative author and subject index in the last issue. It covers human, social, and manpower problems in areas such as employment, retirement, and ethnic and minority group relations. The abstract section is separated into subject areas containing the abstract and full citation; however, there is a separate subject and author index. Gerontology information can be searched using the terms *aged* and *elderly.* The subject and author index is limited to providing only the location number for the abstract.

Index Medicus. Bethesda, Md.: National Library of Medicine.

Primarily an international index for medical information. Includes information on the biological processes of aging and diseases and medical problems of the elderly. It includes a limited amount of information in social gerontology.

Index to Periodical Literature on Aging. Detroit: Lorraine.

Core gerontology journals and other journals that occasionally publish articles of interest to gerontologists are included in this cumulative index to English-language periodicals. The index is arranged alphabetically by subject, with an author index as well as an index to book reviews. The index uses the most specific terms to identify topics on aging and includes cross-references from general to specific terms when required.

International Nursing Index. New York: International Nursing Index.

> The index covers all areas of nursing, as well as information related to hospital administration, health-care delivery services, education, community services, and legislation in relation to health. Although the terms *aging* and *aged* are used, the term *geriatrics* will retrieve specialized information.

Journal of Human Services Abstracts. Rockville, Md.: Project SHARE.

> Published quarterly, the abstract contains all documents in Project SHARE, an automated database. Documents can also be obtained from SHARE. Ordering information is contained within the abstract. There are four sections to the abstract; abstracts, subject index, author index, and an alphabetical list of documents. The abstract section is arranged under major subject areas by order numbers of the documents. The broad term *elderly*, in the subject index, locates information on aging. Information is in all areas of human services for the elderly including needs assessment, health care, adult day care, and nursing homes.

Medical Socioeconomic Research Sources. Chicago, Ill.: American Medical Association.

> Monthly issues of this index cover information in the area of health care and health-care delivery services. It indexes journals, pamphlets, books, theses, and selected government publications. It is one of the few indexes that includes newspaper articles. There is an author and subject index. The term *aging* is primarily used for documents in gerontology and geriatrics; however, information can be retrieved using more specific terms such as *nursing homes* and *pension plans*.

Monthly Catalog of U.S. Government Publications. Washington, D.C.: U.S. Government Printing Office.

> The publications listed in the *Monthly Catalog* include all publications issued from branches of the U.S. government. It is issued monthly and indexes are cumulated semiannually. There is an author, title, subject, and series and reports index in each issue. In the subject index, information in gerontology and geriatrics may be found using the term *aging* with subheadings for more specific topics. Later issues include a key word index.

Public Affairs Information Service Bulletin (PAIS). New York: Public Affairs Information Service.

PAIS Bulletin is a subject index to international English-language public policy literature relating to economic and social conditions, public administration, and international relations. Documents indexed include books, pamphlets, journal articles, government publications, and reports from public and private agencies. The bulletin is published weekly and has a five-year cumulative index. For locating information on aging more specific terms can also be used such as *age and employment, retirement income,* and *longevity.*

Psychological Abstracts. Washington, D.C.: American Psychological Association.

Published monthly, each issue contains an author and a subject index with a separate section for abstracts. The issues are cumulated semiannually at which time the abstracts are combined into two volumes of three months each. Information focuses on the psychosocial and physiological aspects of psychology. The subject index includes only the key words in the title of the document and a code number for locating the abstract and full citation. Aside from using the term *aged* or *elderly,* more specific terms such as *longevity* and *old age* may be used.

Sage Family Studies Abstracts. Beverly Hills, Calif.: Sage.

Published four times a year, the abstract covers books, articles, pamphlets, government publications, theses, and dissertations as well as significant speeches on information related to family studies. The table of contents covers broad areas such as "Family Relationships and Dynamics" and "Family Life Cycle." Included in the abstract is an author and subject index. The subject term lists only the location number of the abstract, all information on the document is contained in the abstract.

Social Sciences Citation Index. Philadelphia: Institute for Scientific Information.

Although this index offers the most information resources, it is significantly different than conventional index services. It consists of three separate, interrelated indexes; the *Citation Index,* the *Source Index* and the *Permuterm Subject Index,* issued quarterly and annually. The index is based on the concept that references used in current articles will refer to earlier material within the same subject area. Detailed instructions for using the index are provided in the beginning of the publication. The *Permuterm*

Subject Index uses the significant word from the title of the article and pairs it with other words in that title. Information on gerontology can be located using the terms *aging, aged,* and *elderly.* Other significant terms related to aging may also be used to retrieve information. Because of the unconventional method of organizing information, it is best to read the detailed instructions for using the index in the front of the publication.

Social Sciences Index. New York: H. W. Wilson.

The focus of the index covers a wide area of the social sciences including environmental sciences, law and criminology, and economics as well as medical services and public administration. The index is arranged alphabetically by author's name and subject term. The term *aged* uses subheadings to list documents under more specific areas such as *adjustment, housing,* and *mental illness.*

Social Work Research & Abstracts. New York: National Association of Social Workers.

Formerly *Abstracts for Social Workers,* this abstract contains articles of original research together with abstracts from various disciplines such as psychology and sociology. It is published four times a year with an annual subject index in the last issue. Information on aging includes areas of health, case management, psychiatric disorders, and widowhood. The content area includes a section on "Aging and the Aged"; however, the subject index provides more extensive information on aging not included in the content area. Complete information on items are obtained through the abstract number provided in the subject index.

Sociological Abstracts. San Diego, Calif.: Sociological Abstracts.

Published five times a year, each issue contains abstracts from documents published during the current year and for approximately four previous years. Journals published by sociological associations as well as those in related areas of economics, education, medicine, community development, and the humanities are included in the abstract. Supplements include abstracts of conference papers. The table of contents list the abstracts under broad categories that include such areas as history and theory of social psychology. For information in gerontology, the best results are obtained using the subject index with the terms *aging* and *elderly*. All items in the subject index use the key terms in the title of the document with an alphanumeric code symbol for locating the citation and abstract.

APPENDIX C

GERONTOLOGY AND GERIATRICS JOURNALS

Activities, Adaptation & Aging. New York: Haworth Press, quarterly.

> The journal focuses on articles concerned with program evaluations, research, and theory in all areas of activities management with the aged. It is aimed at activity directors and coordinators in both community and institutional programs.

Adult Education. Washington, D.C.: Adult Education Association of the U.S.A., quarterly.

> Committed to the dissemination of research and theory in adult and continuing education, the scope of the journal covers research, philosophical analyses, and theoretical aspects of adult education.

Adult Foster Care Journal. New York: Human Sciences Press, Inc., quarterly.

> Coverage in the journal centers on all aspects of adult foster care and presents views of developmental policies, clinical practice, and research on the subject.

African Gerontology. Paris: International Center of Social Gerontology, triannually.

> Published in English and French, information focuses on the status of the elderly in Africa and current research conducted in the field of gerontology.

Age. Omaha, Nebr.: American Aging Association, quarterly.

Articles in *Age* primarily focus on issues in the field of biomedical research. They include topics such as hormones, lipid metabolism, central nervous system, connective tissue, and muscle.

Age and Ageing. London: Bailliere Tindall, quarterly.

The journal is the official journal of the British Geriatrics Society and the British Society for Research on Ageing. Articles in the international journal focus on the clinical, epidemiological, and psychological aspects of medicine and the aged.

Ageing and Society. New York: Cambridge University Press, quarterly.

This is an international journal devoted to publishing contributions to the understanding of human aging, particularly from the viewpoint of the social sciences and humanities.

Ageing International. Washington, D.C.: International Federation on Ageing, quarterly.

Articles in the bulletin cover all aspects of international aging and are published in English, French, Spanish, and German. Special features include a calendar of international conferences.

Aging. Washington, D.C.: Administration on Aging, bimonthly.

Information in the publication focuses primarily on programs at the federal, state, and local levels. Special features include information on aging publications and book reviews.

Aging and Human Development. See *The International Journal of Aging and Human Development.*

Aging and Work. Washington, D.C.: National Council on the Aging, quarterly. (Formerly *Industrial Gerontology.*)

The journal focuses on issues relating to work and aging. The content of the articles is oriented toward factual information about programs and policies affecting middle-aged or older persons and work, and the legal and legislative issues concerning this group.

Aging: Immunology and Infectious Disease. New York: Mary Ann Liebert, quarterly.

The journal focus is on research on immunology and infectious diseases as related to aging. Publications of the journal include basic studies in areas such as host defense mechanisms in animal models and man, alterations in cell interactions, and resistance and response to infections.

Canadian Journal on Aging. Toronto, Canada: Canadian Association on Gerontology, quarterly.

The journal covers a broad range of information on the biological, social science, and social welfare of the elderly in Canada. Articles are written in both French and English.

Clinical Gerontologist: The Journal of Aging and Mental Health. New York: Haworth Press, quarterly.

Designed for use by psychologists, physicians, nurses, social workers, and counselors, the journal focuses on articles that have direct, practical, and clinical importance to multidisciplinary mental-health care teams that work with the elderly in long-term care settings, and community and private practice settings.

Comprehensive Gerontology. Elmont, N.Y.: Munksgaard International, sections A and B triannually, section C annually.

Listed as a new approach to the scientific study of the elderly, the aim and scope of the journal is to contribute to the development of knowledge at all levels. There are three separate sections to the journal. Section A covers clinical and laboratory sciences; section B, the behavioral, social, and applied sciences and, section C, interdisciplinary topics.

Contemporary Long-Term Care. Nashville, Tenn.: Advantage, monthly.

The journal acts as a vehicle for information on all aspects of long-term care. It includes articles on the care and treatment of patients in a variety of settings. There is a section on current news that covers items such as recent legislation and new programs and research.

Educational Gerontology. Washington, D.C.: Hemisphere, quarterly.

Articles in this journal cover academic curricula for adults and continuous adult learning. Information relates to educational programs, as well as the psychological and social factors affecting education and adult learners.

Experimental Aging Research. Southwest Harbor, Maine: Beech Hill, quarterly.

An international and interdisciplinary journal on both human and animal aging in the areas of the biological, biochemical, pharmacological, behavioral, and clinical sciences.

Experimental Gerontology: An International Journal. Elmsford, N.Y.: Pergamon Press, bimonthly.

The focus of the journal is on the international and interdisciplinary scientific study of the biological processes of aging in plants, animals, and humans.

Geriatric Nursing: American Journal of Care for the Aging. New York: American Journal of Nursing, bimonthly.

Information in the journal covers all aspects of nursing care for the elderly, including areas such as nutrition, drugs, death and dying, pain, and health-care policies.

Geriatrics. Duluth, Minn.: Harcourt Brace Jovanovich, monthly.

The publication is aimed primarily toward physicians and medical professionals. Special features include the latest news in geriatric medicine, abstracts from current literature, and brief items on up-to-date information and new frontiers of research in the medical field.

Geriatric Survey. Baltimore, Md.: Williams & Wilkens, bimonthly.

A unique journal that contains abstracts of timely articles from over two hundred journals surveyed. Most of the articles are medically or physiologically oriented, but some are on patient care and social issues concerned with medical practice. The coverage is international in scope.

Gerondontology: An International Journal. Mt. Desert, Maine: Beech Hill, several times a year.

The purpose of the journal is to stimulate dental research in gerontology at both the clinical and scientific level. It offers international and interdisciplinary articles on experimental research and clinical studies.

Gerontion. Calgary, Canada: Gerontion, 5 times per year.

The journal is cited as a vehicle to disseminate information to professionals from all disciplines and health-care settings.

The Gerontologist. Washington, D.C.: Gerontological Society of America, bimonthly.

The focus of the journal is primarily in the area of social gerontology. Articles are interdisciplinary in nature aimed at research and studies. Abstracts of papers presented at the annual meeting of the Gerontological Society are published in a separate issue.

Gerontology and Geriatrics Education. New York: Haworth Press, quarterly.

The primary focus of the journal is on the enhancement of teaching in the field of gerontology and geriatrics at the undergraduate and graduate level. It is intended as a course journal for interdisciplinary programs and curricula.

Gerontology: International Journal of Experimental and Clinical Gerontology. New York: S. Karger, bimonthly.

The journal contains all scientific contributions from the wide field of experimental and clinical studies of the aging process in animals and man.

Home Health Care Services Quarterly. New York: Haworth Press, quarterly.

Aimed at administrators of home-care services, articles from a wide range of disciplines cover research on home health care and alternatives to long-term care for the elderly, disabled, and others who use home-care services. The journal covers research, policy issues, and topics related to training of professionals and paraprofessionals.

The Hospice Journal: The Official Journal of the National Hospice Organization. New York: Haworth Press, quarterly.

The official journal of the National Hospice Organization, it covers a wide array of articles on terminal and palliative hospice care and serves as an interdisciplinary forum for all aspects of care for the dying.

The International Journal of Aging and Human Development. Farmingdale, N.Y.: Baywood, 8 times per year.

Articles in the journal present scholarly research on all aspects of gerontology on an international level. Emphasis is placed on studies and research in the psychosocial area, such as intergenerational relations, institutionalization, social action, and work and retirement.

International Journal of Technology and Aging. New York: Human Sciences Press, semiannually.

The focus of the journal is on the use of appropriate technology for an aging population in areas such as housing design, safety, and rehabilitation.

Journal of Aging and Health. Newbury Park, Calif.: Sage, quarterly.

Dealing with the social and behavioral factors related to aging and health, the journal contains articles from social and behavioral scientists, nursing researchers, demographers, health-service researchers, and allied health professionals.

Journal of Aging and Judaism. New York: Human Sciences Press, quarterly.

The journal acts as a forum for the exchange of both scholarly and practical information. It examines those issues that face the Jewish community in its delivery of services to the elderly.

Journal of Aging and Social Policy. New York: Haworth Press, quarterly.

Acting as a forum for analysis, research, and advocacy of social policy and the aged, the journal aims to generate discussion concerning policy issues faced by a changing society.

Journal of Aging Studies. Greenwich, Conn.: JAI Press.

An international and interdisciplinary journal offering scholarly articles on topics relevant to the aging experience and related to concerns in the social and behavioral sciences.

Journal of Applied Gerontology. Newbury Park, Calif.: Sage, quarterly.

International in scope, the journal covers all aspects of aging practice and policy. A special feature section describes current programs and service and research activities.

Journal of Clinical and Experimental Gerontology. New York: Marcel Dekker.

International in scope, the journal focuses on the biology of aging and its clinical applications. It covers experimental and human gerontology and geriatric medicine for physicians and allied health-care professionals.

Journal of Cross-Cultural Gerontology. Hingham, Mass.: Kluwer Academic, triannually.

An international journal providing a forum for information on the aging process and problems dealing with nonwestern populations, particularly the Third World. It presents research findings, theoretical issues, and applied approaches from the social, economic, historical, and biological perspectives.

Journal of Elder Abuse and Neglect. New York: Haworth Press, quarterly.

Using a multidisciplinary approach, the aim of the journal is to create awareness of abuse and neglect of the elderly, and to provide an understanding of the causes, treatment, effects, and prevention of maltreatment of older persons.

Journal of Geriatric Drug Therapy. New York: Haworth Press, quarterly.

Articles in the journal focus on the clinical use of drugs in older patients relative to therapeutic, pharmacokinetic, toxicologic, and other aspects of drug use.

Journal of Geriatric Psychiatry. New York: International Universities Press, semiannually.

Primarily oriented toward research in psychiatry, this official journal of the Boston Society for Gerontological Psychiatry also contains articles in social gerontology.

Journal of Gerontological Nursing. Thorofare, N.J.: Charles B. Slack, monthly.

Articles in the journal are related to current developments in the field of aging that relate to all aspects of nursing care of the elderly.

Journal of Gerontological Social Work. New York: Haworth Press, quarterly.

The focus of the journal is on social work practice, theory, administration, and consultation in the field of aging. It is oriented toward the practice needs in the social service area.

Journal of Gerontology. Washington, D.C.: Gerontological Society of America, bimonthly.

The journal is primarily research oriented and includes separate sections devoted to the physiological, psychological, and social science areas of gerontology. Selected volumes contain a listing of doctoral dissertations on aging.

Journal of Housing for the Elderly. New York: Haworth Press, quarterly.

The aim of the journal is to present new research in the housing and aging field, as well as to synthesize cross-disciplinary efforts to enhance the residential environments of the elderly.

Journal of Long-Term Care Administration. Bethesda, Md.: American College of Health Care Administrators.

Information in the journal is related to all aspects of the administration of long-term care, including the management of facilities, financial and economic aspects of care, and staffing.

Journal of Minority Aging. Durham, N.C.: National Council on Black Aging, quarterly.

Articles in the journal are devoted to disseminating research on minority aging pertaining to theories and methodologies as they relate to planners and service providers.

Journal of Nutrition for the Elderly. New York: Haworth Press, quarterly.

All aspects of nutrition are covered in the journal including research papers from a variety of fields in the biological and social sciences as they apply to nutrition, community, and long-term care.

Journal of Psychosocial Oncology. New York: Haworth Press, quarterly.

A multidisciplinary journal that focuses on the psychosocial needs of cancer patients and their families. Many of the articles in the journal relate to clinical and research information in the field of oncology as it applies to elderly cancer patients.

Journal of Religion and Aging. New York: Haworth Press, quarterly.

An interdisciplinary and interfaith journal that provides information in the emerging field of religious gerontology. Information centers on theory and applied research on the role of religion and aging, as well as pastoral care. It incorporates the latest research in the field with practical articles for programs in religious institutions.

Journal of the American Geriatrics Society. New York: Elsevier Science, monthly.

Primarily intended for those in the geriatric field, the journal publishes both clinical and basic science studies on a broad range of topics, including medical ethics, law, public policy, and clinical experiences.

Journal of Women and Aging. New York: Haworth Press, quarterly.

A multidisciplinary journal providing publications that focus on issues and concerns of older women, care and services, and research and education.

Lifelong Learning. Washington, D.C.: Adult Education Association of the U.S.A., 8 times per year.

Articles in the journal are intended to bridge the gap between theory and practice with application to the field of lifelong education.

Long-Term Care and Health Services Administration Quarterly. Kansas City, Mo.: American Nurses Association, quarterly.

Concerned with the administrative and clinical practice in long-term care, the quarterly includes information from both gerontological and geriatric research. It focuses on adminstrative problems and finances, staff training, and development of facilities for long-term care.

Omega: Journal of Death and Dying. Farmingdale, N.Y.: Baywood, quarterly.

As a source of information on the issues of dying, death, bereavement, and suicide and other lethal behavior, there are a considerable number of articles concerned with aging and death.

Perspective on Aging. Washington, D.C.: The National Council on the Aging, bimonthly.

The journal contains short factual articles on current topics, legislation, and programs in aging. It also includes public policy reports and NCOA activities.

Physical and Occupational Therapy in Geriatrics. New York: Haworth Press, quarterly.

Articles in the journal provide therapists and others involved in geriatric rehabilitation with the latest information concerning the emerging trends in the clinical management of the geriatric client.

Pride Institute Journal of Long-Term Home Health Care. New York: St. Vincent's Hospital, quarterly.

Current research issues in long-term home health care are the main focus of this journal as well as articles from proceedings and seminars, research findings, and long-term care in the areas of education, training, and service.

Psychology and Aging. Washington, D.C.: American Psychological Association, quarterly.

The publication is concerned with a broad array of psychological and behavioral interest in adult development and aging. Reports of research include applied, biobehavioral, clinical, educational, and experimental areas of psychology.

Research on Aging. Beverly Hills, Calif.: Sage, quarterly.

An interdisciplinary journal that covers a wide scope of study including sociology, geriatrics, history, psychology, anthropology, public health, economics, and social work. Emphasis of the publication is on the cross-disciplinary aspect of gerontology.

Social Security Bulletin. Washington, D.C.: U.S. Government Printing Office.

The focus of the publication is on information concerning the legislative, economic, work, and employment issues related to Social Security benefits. It contains statistical data as well as textual information.

APPENDIX D

SELECTED COMPUTERIZED DATABASES

Ageline

Producer:
> American Association of Retired Persons
> 1909 K Street, NW
> Washington, D.C.

Coverage: 1978 to the present.

Subject Coverage: Information in AGELINE focuses on the social-psychological perspective on issues such as economics, family relationships, demographic trends, political, and health-care issues of middle-aged and older adults. Citations from journal articles, books, government documents, reports, dissertations, and conference papers are included. It also offers description of over two thousand federally funded research projects in aging.

The Architecture Database

Producer:
> British Architectural Library
> 66 Portland Place
> London WIN 4AD
> United Kingdom

Coverage: 1978 to the present.

Subject Coverage: The literature indexed covers areas related to the history, education, practice, and management in architecture. It includes subjects such as housing, interior design, structural elements, and information on a wide variety of building types. Information is derived from more than four hundred current periodicals from over 45 countries.

Corresponding Printed Indexes: Architectural Periodicals Index; Architectural Books.

CANCERLIT

Producer:

National Library of Medicine
8600 Rockville Pike
Bethesda, Maryland

Coverage: 1963 to the present.

Subject Coverage: The scope includes cancer-related articles from a wide variety of sources. It focuses on experimental and clinical cancer therapy, agents that cause cancer as well as the biochemistry, immunology, physiology, and other aspects of cancer.

Corresponding Printed Indexes: Carcinogenesis Abstracts; Cancer Therapy Abstracts.

Clinical Abstracts

Producer:

Medical Information Systems
Reference & Index Services, Inc.
3845 N. Meridian Street
Indianapolis, Indiana

Coverage: 1981 to the present.

Subject Coverage: The database provides access to more than three hundred English-language medical journals, and covers major subject areas such as family practice, internal medicine, general surgery, and cardiovascular surgery.

Donnelley Demographics

Producer:

Donnelley Marketing Information Services

1351 Washington Boulevard, 4th Floor
Stamford, Connecticut

Coverage: 1980 census data, with current-year estimates and five-year projections in selected categories.

Subject Coverage: Information in the database can be searched by geographic levels as well as by demographic characteristics such as education, income, race, age, population, and housing. Data are available for areas in the United States, and for individual state, county, and Standard Metropolitan Statistical Areas (SMSA).

Economic Literature Index

Producer:
American Economic Association
Pittsburgh, Pennsylvania

Coverage: 1969 to the present.

Subject Coverage: The database covers both journal articles and book reviews on all aspects of economics including areas such as work and employment, retirement, pension benefits, and preretirement counseling and programs.

Corresponding Printed Indexes: Index of Economic Articles; index section of the quarterly *Journal of Economic Literature.*

EMBASE (formerly Excerpta Medica)

Producer:
Elsevier Science Publishers
52 Vanderbilt Avenue
New York, New York

Coverage: 1974 to the present (in three database files).

Subject Coverage: Embase is an international source for information in the area of biomedical literature. It covers the entire field of human medicine and related disciplines. The range of topics includes areas such as geriatrics, developmental biology, environmental health, hospital management, and public health.

Corresponding Printed Index: Excerpta Medica.

ERIC

Producer:
> National Institute of Education
> Educational Resources Information Center
> Washington, D.C.

Coverage: 1966 to the present.

Subject Coverage: ERIC covers information resources related to adult education, counseling, and personnel services, and educational management as well as the social and psychological areas. Documents include research and technical reports, conference papers and proceedings, bibliographies, state-of-the-art reviews, dissertations, and journal articles and monographs.

Corresponding Printed Indexes: CIJE (Current Index to Journals in Education); Resources in Education.

Family Resources

Producer:
> National Council on Family Relations
> St. Paul, Minnesota

Coverage: 1970 (nonjournal items); 1973 to the present (journal articles).

Subject Coverage: The database provides bibliographic coverage of the psychosocial literature related to the family in the areas of medicine, psychology, sociology, and education. Documents include journal articles, books, audiovisuals, government publications, instructional material, and human resources.

Food Science and Technology Abstracts

Producer:
> International Food Information Service, Reading,
> Berkshire, England

Coverage: 1969 to the present.

Subject Coverage: FSTA provides access to international information related to food science and technology and related disciplines such as nutrition, chemistry of foods, and agriculture.

GPO Monthly Catalog

Producer:
> Superintendent of Documents
> U.S. Government Printing Office
> Washington, D.C.

Coverage: 1976 to the present.

Subject Coverage: Public documents generated by the legislative and executive branches of the U.S. government and public documents for sale by the Superintendent of Documents are included in the material indexed. A selected group of documents from the judicial branch of the government are also indexed. Some of the major subject areas include health and human services, education, housing, and labor.

Corresponding Printed Index: Monthly Catalog of U.S. Government Publications.

Grants

Producer:
> The Oryx Press
> 2214 N. Central at Encanto
> Phoenix, Arizona

Coverage: current information.

Subject Coverage: Information in the database covers available grants offered by federal, state, and local governments; commercial organizations; associations; and private foundations. The references include application deadlines up to six months ahead, a full description of the grant, qualifications, money available, and renewability together with the name, address, and telephone number for the sponsoring organization.

Corresponding Printed Indexes: Grants Information System (GIS), the quarterly cumulative volumes; *Faculty Alert Bulletin.*

Health Planning and Administration

Producer:
> National Library of Medicine
> 8600 Rockville Pike
> Bethesda, Maryland

Coverage: 1975 to the present.

Subject Coverage: Documents in the database are selected references taken from MEDLINE and the *Hospital Literature Index.* References relate to all aspects of health-care planning, facilities, health insurance, and various aspects of finance, administration, and licensure applying to the delivery of health-care services.

Corresponding Printed Index: Hospital Literature Index.

Management Contents

Producer:
    Management Contents
    2265 Carlson Drive
    Northbrook, Illinois

Coverage: 1974 to the present.

Subject Coverage: The database features comprehensive coverage of topics related to management. It covers all aspects of business management including marketing research, personnel relations, employee benefits, economics, and finance.

MEDLINE

Producer:
    National Library of Medicine
    8600 Rockville Pike
    Bethesda, Maryland

Coverage: 1966 to the present (two files).

Subject Coverage: The database serves as a major source for biomedical literature in areas such as clinical and experimental medicine, dentistry, nursing, psychiatry, and psychology. It also covers additional topics relating to health occupations as well as medical specialties on an international level.

Corresponding Printed Indexes: Index Medicus; Index to Dental Literature; International Nursing Index.

Mental Health Abstracts

Producer:
    IFE/Plenum Data Company

3202 Kirkwood Highway
Wilmington, Delaware

Coverage: 1969 to the present.

Subject Coverage: The database covers international information relating to the general topic of mental health and includes, among other topics, the fields of aging, mental-health services, psychopharmacology, and social issues. It includes journal articles, books, and technical reports as well as workshops and proceedings, and nonprint media.

Nursing & Allied Health

Producer:
CINAHL
P. O. Box 871
Glendale, California

Coverage: 1983 to the present.

Subject Coverage: Information in the database is designed to meet the needs of nursing and allied health professionals. It selects documents from over three hundred English-language journals and primary journals from the allied health disciplines and includes pertinent citations from biomedical journals. Among the areas treated in the database are health education, occupational and physical therapy, and social service in health care.

Corresponding Printed Index: Cumulative Index to Nursing and Allied Health Literature.

PAIS International

Producer:
Public Affairs Information Service, Inc.
New York, N.Y.

Coverage: 1972 to the present *PAIS Foreign Language Index;* 1976 to the present *PAIS Bulletin.*

Subject Coverage: PAIS is an index to public policy literature of business, economics, finance, law, international relations, government, political science, and other social science areas. It includes periodical literature; books; government documents on a federal, state, and local level; and organizational reports.

Corresponding Printed Indexes: PAIS Foreign Language Index; PAIS Bulletin.

PsychINFO

Producer:
> American Psychological Association
> 1200 Seventeenth Street, NW
> Washington, D.C.

Coverage: 1967 to the present.

Subject Coverage: The contents of this database cover international literature in psychology and related areas such as sociology, education, pharmacology, physical and psychological disorders and communications systems. Documents include journal articles, technical and conference reports, monographs, and dissertations.

Corresponding Printed Index: Psychological Abstracts.

Social Scisearch

Producer:
> Institute for Scientific Information
> Philadelphia, Pennsylvania

Coverage: 1972 to the present.

Subject Coverage: A multidisciplinary database that covers items from over 1,500 social science journals and selected items from 3,000 additional journals in the natural, physical, and biomedical sciences. It covers all areas of the social and behavioral sciences.

Corresponding Printed Index: Social Sciences Citation Index.

Sociological Abstracts

Producer:
> Sociological Abstracts, Inc.
> P. O. Box 22206
> San Diego, California

Coverage: 1963 to the present.

Subject Coverage: The database covers information sources in sociology and related disciplines in the social and behavioral sciences on an international level. The documents indexed cover a wide range of publications from journal articles and monographs to conference reports and original research. Information is in areas such as social psychology, demography, community development, the family, social change, and economic development.

Corresponding Printed Index: Sociological Abstracts.

INDEX

About the Authors

DOROTHEA R. ZITO is Director of the Gerontological Research Information Program and Information Consultant at Syracuse University. She has published articles and presented papers on topics in information sciences and gerontology.

GEORGE V. ZITO is Associate Professor of Sociology at Syracuse University. His publications include *Systems of Discourse* (Greenwood Press, 1984), *Population and Its Problems,* and other books, as well as journal articles and contributed chapters.